BEYOND AND WITHIN

Beyond
and Within

The White Eagle Way
to Meditate Effortlessly

White Eagle Books
NWEW LANDS · LISS · HAMPSHIRE · UK

First published Autumn 2022

British Library Cataloguing-in-Publication data
A cataogue record for this book is available
from the British Library

© Copyright, The White Eagle Lodge, 2022

ISBN 978-0-85487-251-0

Editorial Material by Anna Hayward

Printed in the Czech Republic with the
assistance of Akcent Media

Contents

1. Finding Heaven

IF WE ASK ourselves what we actually want in life, the ultimate answer, when we have gone through the superficial and immediate things, might be to become aware that we are greater beings than we think we are; that we are all immortal, and that there is not only compensation for suffering, but such joy that pain ceases to exist.

In some ways such a state could be viewed as heaven; one which is beyond the earthly self, but also, as we shall discover in this book, within us. Indeed, all the pleasure, greed and desire of the world could be seen as an attempt to find happiness – or to see it in its fulfilment, as heaven. This is a largely unrecognized yearning, and it also remains unsatisfied, since none of our bungled attempts at happiness actually lead to an awareness of heaven, merely a momentary illusion of completeness and satisfaction.

White Eagle meditation, sometimes called heaet meditation, is ultimately about finding the level of awareness that could be called heaven. Possibly all meditation has this aim, but for White Eagle the end of meditation is the knowledge of eternal life and of a heavenly state of life which awaits us. Moreover, he assures us that with the right application, we can find this heaven while we are still in our physical bodies. He points to meditation as a means to this end, not only in the meditative state itself, but through the changes that meditation brings about within us. Often these are almost unsought and certainly not obvious, but they gradually create heaven – states of beauty, tranquillity, tolerance, understanding, and even joy – for us right here on Earth, if we let them.

So this book is about finding a state of being which is beyond the physical, but which is also to be found within ourselves, and which is our true home It would be good to keep that thought in mind while practising the exercises and reading about the techniques, because White Eagle meditation goes far beyond simply visualizing something beautiful, or finding a peaceful place, or stilling the clamour of the mind – although all those things are part of it. It goes beyond them to our quite literally becoming aware of heaven. We can get so caught up in the techniques, in the struggle, in the method, that the ultimate purpose gets lost, or is never found. Instead, we need to aim high; to aim for heaven all the time, and especially when it feels elusive. We have to keep reminding ourselves that it is there; believing in it and visualizing it, until suddenly the creation of heaven becomes our absorption into heaven. It can be subtle, but it can also happen in a flash, so we have to be ready for it!

How do we do this, especially if we don't think we've experienced heaven before? That is where meditation techniques come in; they are all designed to help us find heaven. When we decide to go on holiday, we keep in our minds the vision and thought of what we are travelling towards. That carries us through the necessary difficulties of the journey; it keeps us going with the promise of an end which is worth waiting for. When you are using the exercises and getting a grip on the techniques, keep the bigger purpose in mind, not just as an end result, but as a constant companion which can reveal itself at any moment … truly!

What is Beyond and Within?

Heaven is indeed our true home – that place at the spiritual level where our greater self exists, and to which we return after death. At the same time, it is also the place where we meet God within. When we experience another plane of existence in our meditations, we recognize it, not merely visually, but in the depths of our being. That part of us which is linked at all times to our soul responds automatically. The mind can take time to catch up, but the feelings are stirred and even the body.

When we sit to meditate, we are, in a sense, going home to this very basic consciousness of happiness! We are going home to that place of light consciousness in which we truly live. As we meditate, we are creating a path homewards, even if we can't immediately see home. It's as if we are travelling through thick forest and up a steep mountainside. At first the jungle growth seems impenetrable, but gradually, as we trace that path over and over again, we clear the way – until eventually we travel it with ease. Meditation involves a rising in consciousness, a raising of vibrations, so that we come out onto the top of the 'hill', above the jungle, and are able to see with clear vision the route we have travelled and the road ahead.

This does not always happen in a way that's obvious to the earthly senses, and even when we have been meditating for years, there are days and times when it seems that the jungle is impossibly thick and the hilltop far distant! But however much the limited self tells us we cannot do it, the soul is making great strides forward through continual practice, and the way of the heart is expanding within us.

There's no waste when we are aspiring.

Heaven, like beauty, is also in the eye of the beholder – or, we might say, the soul – which means it is different for each one of us. White Eagle says: 'The ordinary souls of ordinary people, the dear humanity we love for their kindliness, may not know much about spiritual law. They are, however, kind to one another. People are like that. Always when they come into contact with their fellow creatures they are ready to do a kindness. After death such ordinary people pass quickly through the lower astral in a kind of dreamlike state, sometimes without awakening, until they reach the higher astral plane. There they again meet their friends, not only of the incarnation they have just finished but sometimes companions of former incarnations. It is really a plane of reunion where the soul enjoys an enhanced life, continuing the many different interests such as music and art, literature and perhaps science which it enjoyed when on earth. It will be drawn to its particular interest in this higher astral world and will enjoy new freedom and opportunity of learning more of the particular subject which attracts it. Intense joy can come to the musician as the soul experiences without limitation the joys of music – and the same applies to art.

'We will try to show what we mean. You may love music and yet be unable to express yourself in your present life. On the astral plane that desire will be granted. You will stand before an instrument and find that you can play the instrument without limitation. The music that was longing for expression in your soul would find expression through whatever instrument you like best – a piano, a stringed instrument or whatever you choose. Or, if you longed to take part in an orchestra or in a choir, you would find yourself a member and that you were as good a musician as anyone else there.

The same thing applies with pictures. You long to paint, you long to create beauty; on the astral plane all limitations fall away and the soul expresses itself in colour, form or music exactly, perfectly. These things bring intense happiness.'

'Every country has its replica in spirit, and each has its own temple of spiritual power. There are planes of spirit, also, where those of particular religions go: the Roman Catholic community, for example, or the Anglican community, the Buddhist community and so on. But these planes exist close to the earth. The temples of spiritual enlightenment, however, have a different work to do.'

Bringing Heaven to Earth Effortlessly

Repetition is necessary for anything we wish to learn, but there is a reminder of the subtitle of this book, 'The White Eagle Way to Meditate Effortlessly', in all White Eagle has said about the importance of 'being', rather than 'doing'. This applies as much – if not more – to meditation as to living. People see life as being about striving, about getting something right or wrong, about aims and goals and efficiency and about being purposeful in a planned way. Spiritual teaching down the ages, however, has stressed the importance of quiet attention, 'letting go and letting God'.

Much of this book, therefore, is about ways to trust that we are spiritual beings, and as such are guided by our greater self. The greater self is the same as the God within us. We cannot go wrong if we surrender, at all times, to that God within.

It is however true to say that what we experience of heaven inwardly has an effect on our outward lives. The awareness is like a vibration which resonates at the inner level. Because all life is one, that vibration also echoes in our bodies and minds, sets us dancing to a new tune. As we have experienced, so we become. White Eagle has a few things to say about this:

'While you live in your physical body, you are imprisoned – to a degree but not entirely – and you find great difficulty in holding this picture of life at that high level. From that level right down to the earthly, the physical level, are many interpenetrating planes. It is impossible to isolate any one plane, or for anyone to isolate him or herself on any plane because your life is ever interwoven with the whole of life. This may sound to you a simple statement, but it is one of the fundamental truths, and you must come to understand this interweaving of all the kingdoms of life.'

'When you can rise in consciousness to contact these higher realms, you touch a real heaven world, and receive into your being the beautiful influences from that world. The temple of the spirit may seem to be individual; it may be universal; and this same temple can be seen by every soul when its eyes are opened.'

'By dwelling in God you enter into God's harmony and so become a channel for harmony. Therefore harmony flows through you and it cannot help but recreate harmonious conditions. Become attuned to the gentle spirit of God and love and light. Then your life will become harmonious. *Seek ye first the kingdom of heaven and all things shall be added unto you.* Not because you want certain things to happen, but simply because you love God. God is certain to manifest. The manifestation of God through the physical body will manifest as healthiness and beauty and it must manifest in everything around you. You create heaven on earth. Seek ye first …God. Only God – only the light. Think of nothing else.'

'One of the greatest helps to you on your journey in search of God (and this is the purpose of your life) is meditation. Books will not get you there, although they can point the way; words will not get you there. You have to take the journey yourself. You have to experience for yourself those higher states of consciousness, the reality of the inner world. This can begin for you in the practice of meditation. With your first contact with the universal life through meditation, something happens to you which has never happened before.'

Imagining your own Heaven

Firstly, think about the kind of environment which makes you feel in touch with spiritual things: is it among trees, in a temple or small chapel, in mountains, or in a garden?

Create a place like this in your mind, or rather in your imagination: a place beyond the physical. White Eagle would call it the etheric. In this place, at this moment, you feel you would be most able to be at one with your true spirit.

In your imagination, find a spot there where you can lie – or sit, kneel, or stand – and open wide your arms and your heart to your greatest self, to your spiritual essence.

Imagine the greater part of your soul existing in that place, and the positive energies flowing to you in your physical body and personality.

What would you most want to learn from your spirit? Imagine that happening. What would be said?

Whatever your need at this moment, allow yourself to receive it from heaven. What you are in touch with is the most exact and effective transforming or sustaining power.

So finding heaven is not merely about experiencing a more beautiful place. Heaven is also something which becomes real within – it is a change of consciousness. It is a state of mind which can be found at any time. In the next chapter we will explore this more.

The Transforming Archway of Light

You are standing before an archway filled with light. Through this archway is the positive sphere of heaven, and this entrance is a transforming portal. This means that as you step between the pillars, what we call negative states of mind and feeling are transmuted into their opposite: dullness of mind becomes clarity, heaviness of body becomes lightness and freedom of movement. Sadness and depression become joy.

Stand in the archway and feel the light flowing down, over and through your whole being. Allow the transformation to take place, as a butterfly accepts the shedding of its chrysalis. Imagine how different you would feel when you step forwards through the portal and out into the sunlight.

2. What is Consciousness?

WHEN WE are thinking about such things as subtle energies and what one might call 'heaven', the question cannot help but arise, 'What is consciousness?'. This is a question that philosophers and scientists, not to mention the medical profession, are busy right now exploring and debating. For instance, medical scientists have reason to believe that a person in a coma may be more conscious than was previously believed, and are redoubling their efforts to find ways to help someone who may still be aware, but unable to move or communicate. Here, in effect, we have a possibility that consciousness may be separate from the body in some way, even separate from usual brain activity.

When we meditate, it's thus conceivable that we might be deliberately plugging in to levels of consciousness which are independent of the earthly body and mind, or even into the state of consciousness which we believe we inhabit when the physical body is dead. One can only hope that in some way those who are in a coma can find their way to that state, so that they may no longer feel trapped. In the teaching that follows, White Eagle describes how all states of consciousness interpenetrate, as well as the journey we take through them and back:

'We have told you about certain glorious states of consciousness to which human beings can attain. You are aware that as you sit here you are conscious, if you wish, of your body. If you want to reach out, you can be conscious of your emotional body. That is, your emotions become stirred and your desires active. This quickens the astral state of life, which is governed by feeling, by emotion. Then again you can reach out above the emotions; you can by an effort of will become active on the mental plane. You can even go beyond that mental conception when the higher emotions come into operation and you become conscious of a heavenly state.

'So when you sit to meditate upon spiritual things you usually go through this process of being first conscious of the body (which can be very troublesome until, by your will, you control this body). Then your feelings become active, perhaps stimulated by music or by words. Now you are being raised in consciousness, but you are still within yourself. Step by step you go through the varying states of consciousness to the mental and the heavenly. When you once reach the heavenly state, although you are still fully aware of your inner being, of your higher self or your soul, you are also aware of heavenly things. This is made clear to you first of all by light. You feel lighter, more radiant. Something in you activates the physical vehicle, the nervous system. You experience a telepathic communication between the heavenly self or the heavenly state of consciousness and your body. In the degree you become aware of the body you feel a heaviness, the pull of the earth.

'This is because you have both stimulated that heavenly consciousness and also linked the heavenly with the earth life. So in time you become pulled back. Yet the one life contains all these states of consciousness. What happens when you are unable to sustain life in the body any longer? Then the spirit withdraws and death takes place, the body being only an envelope or clothing to the spirit. But you still remain exactly the same as when you have a body attached to your soul and spirit.'

Aware on Many Levels at Once

In meditation, then, we can be present on many levels at once. We recognize the physical, but can be aware of other levels of consciousness at the same time. It's a bit like when we are driving and we can sense in peripheral vision what is happening alongside the car, but also be aware of the road in front, and at the same time feel the sensation of changing gear with foot and hand.

What we do in meditation is take our main focus away from the physical, as much as we can, so that the spiritual has our greatest attention. In the driving analogy, that's the road and the car in front. White Eagle says,

'Now we would like to refer again to the illusion of time and space. Space is an idea in the mind or in your consciousness (time also is only in your consciousness), as you will discover in your meditation classes. You may, for instance, think back for ten thousand years, and relive a life of the far past. People say, "It is all rubbish; it is impossible to recall what you did on earth ten thousand years ago". But they are wrong, because memories of experiences which affect the soul remain within the soul's consciousness forever and can be relived at will. There is no question of time lag; all is the Eternal Now. All is a question of consciousness, of awareness of life and of God. When you meditate on God, you automatically feel that you are rising into the heights, because at your stage of development you think of good or God as being above you. So you rise into the light at the apex of the mountain and there you are bathed in this eternal light. You feel within your heart harmony and love. You know then that you are in "It", a part of "It", and there is no past, no future, no height and no depth. You are in a dimension which your mathematicians have not yet resolved, but it is a state of supreme or cosmic consciousness.'

'You are perhaps aware that the astral plane, the etheric, the mental, the celestial – all these planes – interpenetrate. Yet you cannot understand what this means, being so limited by a mental conception as to the nature of space and time.'

The Other Part of the Self – A Meditation

As you sit to meditate, you may still be aware of discomfort in your body or anxiety or confusion in your mind, but within and beneath all of this physical sensation is something greater. Feel it now as a deeper stillness; perhaps imagine it as a warm light which is within every part of you; every cell, every thought, every feeling…. This is an essence which is pervading all and which is the greatest power and the greatest wisdom, but most of all the greatest love. Allow your focus to dwell on this warm light, on this transcendent sensation.

Feel this divine essence as a deeper part of all the sensations you are now experiencing, a deeper part of your breathing … of any physical awareness you have, of any emotion, of any thought…. So although you may still be aware of all these, you keep your attention on this other part of yourself; the part which animates all….

This power, wisdom and love is part of your being, but is not held by any of the emotional, mental and physical challenges. Feel the deep peace and stillness of this light; this higher form of love, allowing you to gaze at any physical pain, any difficult emotion, any mental disturbance with a detached awareness. As you do this, you will gain perspective, understanding and a sense of freedom. You may not be aware of this at first. Try not to grab for the experience, just rest in this part of the self which is beyond physical sensation, and trust the divinity within.

When you return to the outer world you will carry within your consciousness an awareness that at any point in time, with whatever you are concerned with, with whatever emotion or thought grips you, this other part of you exists within it all – balancing, transforming, bringing a transcendent love to bear.

3.
Trusting the Process of Meditation

MEDITATION needs to be a process we can trust, and we need to trust ourselves when meditating. It helps to trust that there is no single right end product, but instead it is a process through which we develop over time, and there is no completion time, only a continual growth. The process of meditation is organic and therefore changes with circumstance; we learn to go with the flow.

The process of meditation is approached and used differently by each individual, depending on where each one begins and on our own soul's need. Furthermore, each one of us is a participant in the process, not an empty vessel. The process of meditation therefore relies on us being open, receptive, adaptable, unrestricted, but aware of the procedure which optimizes the highest form of meditative experience.

The benefits of meditation can be to decrease stress, improve mental and emotional control, develop the soul senses, and a lot more, but the purpose of White Eagle meditation goes far beyond the usual ones quoted. White Eagle would say it is to develop the Christ consciousness. Each one becomes their own medium, in that the conditions are created whereby the spirit can reveal itself to the soul, the personality and the body. 'Some might call this Christ consciousness the I AM, which uses the intuitive faculty to make itself known: "I AM the true vine" says Christ;

and the I AM is within you as the flame, the spark which must manifest through love.' This purpose distinguishes White Eagle meditation from stress-releasing relaxation, from what is called mindfulness, and from visualization, though all of these form part of the process.

Heart Meditation

White Eagle meditation is freqently referred to as Heart Meditation, which means that our focus is on the particular vibrations which are given and received through the heart chakra, and what he refers to as 'the mind in the heart'. Here is the highest manifestation of divine love, or the I AM. At the heart centre we have a link between heaven as a state of consciousness towards which we aspire, and heaven within – the Christ consciousness of which White Eagle speaks.

White Eagle Heart Meditation does not in any way deny the existence and importance of the other chakras (the centres of spiritual receptivity and energy). White Eagle explains it in this way: 'The pivot of all these centres … is the heart, which is like the sun of your universe. The heart centre in a person is the sun of their universe. The heart chakra breathes in and it breathes out. It absorbs, it takes in sunlight. This is the white light and can be absorbed through all these sensitive or power centres, but chiefly through the centre most harmonious to the Christ love – the heart.

'Now when the spiritual forces are flowing into the heart centre (you will here see the importance of love in all communications – love and harmony and truth), when the love or the spiritual force is flowing into the heart centre at times of great spiritual ecstasy and prayer, that force flows on into the other chakras and they light up.'

'In the method of meditation that we are unfolding we are imparting a way by which you can bring into oper- ation the true spiritual life which is within. A healer can impart to a patient and a teacher to a pupil a degree of help, but the patient or the pupil must work for themselves. Meditation is a path that must be faithfully pursued by the meditator. It may take years, a whole lifetime, or indeed a number of lifetimes in the body for the pupil to reach the goal. You cannot hurry this process. It is necessary to keep on keeping on patiently, but a great deal of time can be wasted when you are not conversant with the true purpose for which you work.'

It is obvious to everyone that the process behind White Eagle's Heart Meditation is a spiritual one. This means that it cannot be totally understood by the mind of earth, but it is felt in the heart. When we experience the process it 'feels' true, but that feeling may not be quantifiable or expressible in words. The process of meditation relies, pri- marily, on the inner core, which is trust not in the mind, but in the Christ light within us as our guide.

In White Eagle meditation the procedure we follow is a sequence, set out below. However, as we will explore later, there is not always a linear progress through the sequence nor do we always go through every one of these stages to any marked degree. Typically, the stages might be:

- Resting, becoming centred and using the breath
- Raising the awareness to the highest plane we can
- Focusing and creating at a level beyond the physi- cal, using the imagination

- Experiencing with the inner senses
- Sending out the light
- Coming back to awareness of the physical
- Grounding and sealing.

The Distinctive Qualities of the White Eagle Meditation

Aspiration to the highest level of awareness is always the first object of White Eagle's meditation training. His teaching on the power of thought demonstrates how this aspiration, which is a deliberate change in the focus of our thinking, raises the consciousness.

The focus is always on beauty and on a heart-centred approach. This focus changes our own vibrational body, so that we not only raise our consciousness to the highest, but become a magnet for the most perfect love to reflect in physical form. It also means that we are not forcing, or judging our progress, but rather acknowledging the challenges inherent in living as a spiritual being in a material world, yet trusting that that spiritual world exists.

There is an element of service or healing incorporated at some point in each meditation. When we reach to the highest plane of love we touch infinite compassion and the will to serve all life. On any level it is natural to give when we love. Fundamental is an understanding of the importance of the imagination, both in creating and becoming aware at subtle, spiritual levels.

The six-pointed star, which the White Eagle meditation uses, is an ancient wisdom symbol of man–woman made perfect in matter and of earthing the spirit. It is a symbol of that Christ consciousness, the I AM mentioned by White

Eagle, which when we reach 'heaven' is more fully embodied within us and shining from us. It is also the focus from which we send out the light.

Our sealing ritual is designed to support the nervous system and balance our sensitivity; this and the careful raising of the consciousness, and bringing back to physical awareness, brings safety to the whole approach. The sealing ritual (see p. 235) is often described as a vibration of love through which only love can pass.

In the White Eagle meditation there are elements of a number of spiritual traditions, but they form a coherent practice. They include:

* the Christian tradition, through aspirational prayer and the Christ light
* the Buddhist, through stillness, mindfulness tradition, dispassion
* Vedic (Hindu) tradition through focal points and mantra
* Tibetan and Zen tradition
* Spiritualist practice, through development of the inner senses and contact with angels and guides
* Native American practices, through focus on the natural world
* Egyptian/Atlantean religion, through focus on the light and the sun
* Taoism, through present-centredness and going with the flow – not pushing. The subtitle of this book is an example: *wuwei* or effortless effort
* Yogic tradition, through the use of the breath and circulation of prana and through the understanding that we are not separate from God
* Lastly, this meditation practice is part of a comprehen-

sive philosophical framework and tradition given to us in the White Eagle teaching, taught and practised over many years.

4. No Travelling Required!
Practising the Presence of God

GOD IS ALL around and within all things. When meditating, we can feel this energy – and at the moment we feel it, there is a sense of release. Something happens inwardly which is like bathing in comfort, reassurance and all the emotions which are the opposite of fear or anxiety or depression.

'It is a wonderful thing, life; it is wonderful to have been breathed forth from the heart of God; to be held in the thought of God, in the mind of God! Yet everything and everyone in Creation is held in the divine Mind. Can you comprehend the extent, the grandeur, the power, the glory of that Mind which creates and holds the creative thought so that that thought becomes a living thing? No; it is beyond the finite mind's power to grasp. Some of you who are accustomed to meditation might have a fleeting conception of this profound truth.'

How often when we meditate we feel we have to get somewhere! To travel to find heaven, stillness, a vision, an understanding … yet White Eagle is saying that we are within God-consciousness already. Poor brain, it has to have a way of interpreting the world in some kind of dimension! Yet spiritually there is no up or down, in or out. Therefore in entering different levels of consciousness, we have to give the brain directions, when really there are none! So, we use the sense of rising, or going inward, to help the brain interpret the change of consciousness. What we are really doing in meditation is practising the presence of God - realizing God within and around us at all times. We are realizing heaven within.

'What humanity is seeking is manifesting in life everywhere. Do not try to separate matter from God, nor yet matter from spirit. Matter is created by spirit and matter in all forms is the result of the working or the development or the life of spirit, or God. Some people feel closer to God in a garden, on the moors or the mountains.'

'God is in everything. The God life is expressed in every form of matter on your earth. Think of life as one great unity. God is in everything, you are in everything; but you do not know it yet. The consciousness has to expand until the spirit within becomes conscious, not only of God but of all God's life…. Let us remember that every particle of our being, whether physical, mental, astral or spiritual, is likewise a part of God, the Infinite. We are not related to God merely through our spirit, for the spirit permeates every atom of the physical body also. We cannot then separate God's essence from the physical body, nor yet from anything that is on God's earth, nor in the heavens.'

The God Within and Within which we Live

If you were asked, 'What is the God within your own being?' how would you reply?

Take a moment now and close your eyes and let that question rest in your mind without resistance to it.

Breathe your resistance away and be open to whatever emerges. How does God within manifest?

No matter what is happening, all around you and within you is an intelligent, loving presence which knows how things are and what soul choices have been made: an all-powerful presence which holds you and upholds you through all things.

Close your eyes again and take your attention to the flow of the life force within you as you breathe. Feel that you sit at the centre of a sphere of consciousness, and that consciousness flows all around you and through you. It doesn't matter what it looks like; just imagine it is there, and if you imagine it as light, energy, divine essence, colour, peace, joy, or simply breath, that is fine … whatever comes to you is how it is for you. All that is required is that you keep bringing your thoughts back to this awareness, which may change as the seconds pass.

At this moment you are aware of how God, the light, the divine consciousness, is the motivating and life-giving essence of your life. It is not something separate from you, or a distant goal, and it is in all life and links you with all life.

This awareness could lead to any kind of meditation, so just go with what works for you, but if you wish, expand your thoughts into the space around you physically, feeling this connection with everything as the life force flows through all, and then include what you wouldn't perceive with physical senses. What are you connected with at a subtle, spiritual level?

This is one awareness which can immediately transform our daily life. To have understood for a moment that

God – the light, spirit, love – is something which is constant around and within us is to be able to live more fearlessly, knowing that God upholds us and sustains us without let up, and no matter what state we are in. In fact, because it is infinite compassion, when we are at our 'worst', God is closest to us in a way which can hardly be understood, and is the opposite of how people can be in the world.

This means that when we meditate, the most effective way to touch otherness within ourselves is simply to remember: to focus, to give it our attention. In meditation we are simply giving our attention to a part of ourselves and of life which exists around and within us all the time, like the breath. It requires no effort, only a change of focus from outward things to inner things, just as we do when we focus on our breath. In fact, effort can be counterproductive, just as forced breathing practice can cause us to become tense rather than relaxed.

'The purpose of man's life is to grow towards consciousness of his own inner God qualities and God glory. The way to do this, put very simply, is continually to rise in thought to the spheres of light, continually to prove receptive to the constructive forces and to the creative power of God.'

God-Breathing Practice and Expansion of Consciousness

Sit quietly somewhere, close your eyes and rest your hands in your lap, palms upwards. Be aware of those hands on your lap. Feel the sensation of the clothing material on the backs of your hands. Imagine your etheric body extending just beyond the physical into another realm. So your hands, the etheric fingers, and the arms extend beyond the sensation of cloth and air, into the world of spirit, of God. What beauty would you touch there?

As you breathe consciously, be aware of your whole aura extending outwards into that serene place of light and love. You breathe in the sweet air of heaven, and if you were to open your inner eyes, you would see loveliness, you would hear harmony, and you would feel a serenity which comes from knowing the true nature of life. Breathe in that feeling of contentment.

Come back gently to awareness of your hands in your lap, your clothing touching them and the rest of your body as it touches the earth. Nothing has changed outwardly, but your consciousness has expanded and you have touched the heaven which is not separate, but is a usually invisible part of our existence.

5. Remembering
Who we Really Are

AS SPIRITUAL beings we have a natural yearning towards
and recognition of spirituality in all its forms, whether it
be, for example, through the natural world, through love
(of any kind), through ritual or music, or through beauty.
However, daily physical life does get in the way of us being
conscious of our spiritual nature, and the spiritual nature
of life as a whole. What this can mean for our meditation
practice is that it feels unnatural, time-wasting, rather than
fruitful, and we can't quite believe in the reality of what
we experience in that time. White Eagle has much to say
about who we really are:

'We would have you forget that you are men and wom-
en. Try to realize that you are spirit, and in the presence of
a large company of spirits, radiant beings and angels. Some
day the heavy curtain between matter and spirit will be dissolved; and while the human being will still be clothed in a
body of flesh for its particular work on the outermost, the
material, or earthly plane, it will no longer be blinded by its
body of flesh; it will be free to come and go as it wills. The
transit from and return to the physical body and the spirit
worlds will be easy. This is a lesson which you are learning
now in this very heavy, dark condition of earth, in which
you feel very depressed at times, and wonder if life is really
worthwhile. It is not worthwhile for what you gather from
the material conditions and the materiality of life, but it is

indeed worthwhile for what you are learning in your soul: the wonderful wisdom, the eventual mastery of the heavenly worlds, even now gradually being absorbed into your consciousness. When, in future days, you choose to reincarnate on earth, you will as a result do so with a full consciousness of what you are doing, and why you are doing it, and with the door between the heaven world from which you descend open, so that you can easily, during sleep, during meditation, pass through that door and rejoin the friends whom you have left behind in spirit.'

'Our Elder Brethren want you continually to remind yourself that you are divine, you are spirit. Cultivate your inner life, your spiritual life, your life of love, thoughtfulness, and any kind action on behalf of your companions that will save them pain and trial, suffering and unhappiness. This means that your soul is constantly working for spiritual ends, no matter what is going on at the earthly level. Therefore, one thought of God, goodness, divine love, will be like switching on a light in a dark place, to which all that is "of the light" will be instantly attracted. This is what our thoughts of God do when we first sit to meditate.'

White Eagle was once asked: 'Is the whole point of meditation that one may contact the true and eternal within so that all suggestions affecting one's life are true suggestions?' And he replied: 'Exactly. That is the reason why in meditation we always advise or suggest the contact first – always first – with the highest, with God the Supreme and Glorious One, with the jewel within the lotus. *Seek ye first the kingdom of God and all these things will be added unto you.*'

'It is very difficult for you to recognize that you are not the little "you" that you think you are – that you are part of a more beautiful soul than you can conceive. That soul

is your true self. Thus only a small part of you is here functioning through your body, while your inner self is attached
at all times to that greater self.'

'The soul is the individuality, the individual consciousness, that part of a person which finds expression through
the mind. The soul does not incarnate in entirety. I give
you the symbol of the triangle. I am going to use that symbol inverted – recall the triangle on its apex, coming down
into the triangle resting on its base, the two of which when
interpenetrated signify the spirit manifesting in matter.
Visualize the triangle descending with only the point penetrating the life of a person. So we find that the greater part
of the triangle remains in the higher realms, in its spiritual
home. The greater self has not entered into physical consciousness, but only the apex is in contact with the brain
of a person.'

Although only part of the soul is in incarnation – as
White Eagle says, like the point of a triangle in contact
with the brain of a person – there is another dimension of
each one of us which is present whilst we are in a material
form. That aspect is the I AM White Eagle referred to earlier; the Christ consciousness which is in every heart. That
is the divinity within. Although we are growing our soul
through successive lifetimes, we always retain the divine
spark, and as we remember who we really are and bring
that greater awareness to bear in our daily encounters, so
that divine spark becomes a sun which radiates from us,
and into which we eventually return, like 'the dewdrop
slipping into the shining sea'. Buddhists call this enlightenment or illumination.

'Souls are like drops in the ocean or grains of sand on
the seashore. Yet each is individual. Each is a unit, but all

blend together, making one grand whole. Many people fear that when they reach that high level of spiritual life they will lose their identity in God, but this is a mistake. God has created you, His son or daughter. He has created you as His child. Of course, you are a part of God. But you have been given an individual spirit. So when you unite with all the spirits, with the great family of God, you are still an individual and retain your own identity. You will not lose that identity. We would raise you in spirit until you feel in the great silence and stillness that cosmic life and at-one-ment. This is the meaning of what your Christian church calls the atonement. It is the love of the cosmic Christ raising all men and women to that level of at-one-ment. It is the love of Christ in you which causes you to attain a degree of spirituality in which you comprehend God's love.'

'Whatever your need, be it physical, spiritual, or material, meditate on this God within, the God which prompts you to love, to act from the very highest motives. You will generate that light. It will vibrate through your vital body, surrounding you with a great light. It will direct its beams along life's pathway. You will not lack anything you need; moreover, you will be an instrument to lighten the life of every man, woman and child you encounter.'

Watching the Waves

As you prepare with gentle awareness of the breath, feel the rise and fall of your chest, as well as the expansion and retraction of the rib cage. This is a wave-like motion which is so natural and easy, just like the waves flowing onto a beach and retreating back. As you feel this movement of your body, perhaps you will see in your mind's eye an expanse of golden sand and a blue-green sea stretching to the horizon. With each breath, the white-capped waves roll in and out, while the earth is still, receiving the blessing and giving it back to the ocean.

Have the feeling that what you are watching and feeling is the breath of God within you. It is the flow of prana, chi or light, which continuously fills your life, and can pass from you in blessing and healing to all.

6. Simply Breathe

WHILE WE ARE in a physical body, the breath is most of the time unconscious and therefore uncontrolled, but it can also be consciously controlled. It doesn't, however, cease. When we breathe in and breathe out consciously, we simply bring our attention to a natural process which is happening all the time. The breath is the link between the conscious and the unconscious, between the nervous system and the etheric body; and, as such, all the energies both spiritual as well as physical are influenced by and controlled by the breath.

In the Hindu and Tibetan Buddhist traditions the root words to do with the subtle energies in the body are linked with the word 'wind', in the sense that the wind conveys to our minds the idea of motion. With the breath, nothing is static, fixed or rigid, and thus an aspect of it is bringing about change. The breath flows – it flows even when we are asleep or in a coma – and the air we breathe passes through countless places and states and enters many different forms of life, allowing them to transform and to grow.

The practice of *pranayama* (mindfulness of the breath), both in the Yogic tradition and in White Eagle's, is therefore more than the simple art of breathing consciously or deeply; it is a way of effecting change at a profound psychological and soul level, one which can transform the way in which we live our lives. Yet we do not have to know the deeper meaning of *pranayama* in order to find out what the breath can do. A simple practice of conscious breathing can bring us to a state of consciousness in which we know something of God at an inner level, something which is hard to describe. There is a way in which we move beyond the physical breathing, in and out, into a realm where we are freer than the wind.

At the Centre of the Wind:
the Seed Atom in the Heart

White Eagle teaches us:

'The pivot of all the centres in the evolved type of human being is the heart, which is like the sun of your universe. The heart centre is the sun of the human universe. The heart chakra breathes in and it breathes out. It absorbs, it takes in sunlight. The physical sun is, shall we say, the body or vehicle of the Lord Christ. The ancients did not worship the sun, as is often stated; the sun worshippers of old were taught to worship the Sun Spirit, thought to abide in the sun, the spirit of goodness and love, the influence of which came into man's heart. So each being takes in from the light. As the physical sun sustains life in the body, so the spiritual light and warmth behind that sun sustains the spiritual life in humans.'

'Stand if possible before an open window. As you inhale each breath, aspire to God – feel that God is entering into you; as you exhale, bless all life. This inbreathing will cause spiritual light, the spiritual sun behind the physical sun, to enter into you and register on the membranes at the head centre, on the brow; and from that centre mentally you can direct the light to the heart centre to bring spiritual water and sunlight to the which rests in the human heart.

'Do this each day if you can, if you are sufficiently enthusiastic and keen on your wellbeing. Do it for as long as you can and like, but without strain.'

Just as the wind, through its movement, can create a vortex, so after a period of conscious breathing, you forget the mechanics of what you are doing and you find yourself at a still centre. The breath now becomes unconscious again, having done its work to bring you to a place where there is poise, centredness, detachment.

However, this is not unfeeling; it is not cold, but it is a level of consciousness which is detached from the body and mind and emotions of the earth, and instead in harmony with a state of being which sees beyond these things. In other words, you might say it is a state of heaven, of being where God is. God breathes you. You might still be aware of your body, mind and emotions, but they no longer have the power to affect you – they arise and they go away. Your consciousness resides at that still centre of your being where you are connected with all things, and where the comfort, warmth, love, sustenance and the peace of God is.

White Eagle says: 'If you can sit quietly and breathe in the peace of God, you can feel then that you will be raised in consciousness. And you will begin to see form or colour or life at a higher level of vision. And as surely as night follows day, you will know that you have within yourself something which is related to all: not only form of life, colour and sound which is radiating all around you, but which is around you in all people. If you will sit in peace and quiet in meditation and just try to realize or imagine this life, this life of spirit, life in a higher ether all around you, you will feel that you are part of it. That is the point – you are part of "It", you are part of the Whole. We have often said to you, "in love there is no separation". Of course not, because love is God, and when you love you are with God, and God is in all life, all peoples. Never forget this relationship between yourself and the Great Spirit.'

'Breathing has the effect of harmonizing the channel to the divine, to God, to the innermost, the centre within. By slowing down the breathing and breathing the God life, the whole being is harmonized, and the Divine Energy is brought into being. Breathing can link up the three centres – the heart, the throat and the head. When the three centres are brought into complete attunement, perfect harmony exists and then the projection goes forth with great power. And as the projection goes forth, let it do so on a breath of God. You breathe in Divine Energy, you breathe out or project the breath of God, the divine breath, to bless and to heal.'

'Few, if any, breathe out sufficiently. Most people pant. You may not think you do, but many people breathe only with the top of the lungs, leaving an accumulation of poison in the lower part of the lungs. This may go on for the whole lifetime. One should learn then to breathe deeply. But you won't do it without application. You must breathe slowly, quietly, harmoniously; gradually getting the breath deeper until you are filling and emptying the lower part of the lungs and expanding the ribs as you breathe. It must come gradually. Try this exercise by taking six of these breaths each morning.'

Conscious Breathing

The technique that follows can be undertaken as a regular practice, but the beauty of it is that it can also be employed quickly in situations where one feels the need for calm. In THE BREATHING BOOK, the yoga teacher Donna Farhi refers to a similar version of the practice, which she in turn has adapted from Carola Spreads' book, WAYS TO BETTER BREATHING. It has been known for some time that deeper breathing techniques can have a powerful restorative and calming effect on many aspects of the body. Donna Farhi relates how the effects of 'straw' breathing, as it is called, are even greater.

For this exercise you can either be sitting or lying down on your back. You need to be comfortable, but the firmer the surface you can tolerate lying on, the better. The firmness actually allows the muscles of the back to relax more than a soft surface, and also gives the lungs room to expand. When you lie down, do so with your arms a short way out from your sides and the palms upwards, and with something under your head so that it does not tilt backwards. If you are sitting, it is helpful to be upright in a chair, with cushions behind your back if you need support, rather than slouched, again so that the muscles can relax in as upright a position as possible without strain and the chest is free to move.

If at any time you begin to feel emotionally uncomfortable, then stop and take your mind off your breathing. This reaction may particularly apply to anyone who has had a problem with their breathing, for example, if you suffer from asthma. If in doubt at all about this, contact your healthcare practitioner for advice.

To begin the exercise, experience the sensation of the letting go of tension. There is a particular spot halfway between the skull and the shoulders. It is in the middle of the neck. Think of that spot becoming limp and loose, and this will also enable the shoulders and the brow to relax. There may be a feeling of release with your breathing as well, like a sigh, when this happens. Imagine yourself surrounded by warmth, peace and contentment.

Just through your doing this, the breathing will naturally deepen without effort, and the whole point of this breathing routine is that it is without effort. The only attention you pay is to how you hold your lips. Adopt the position of the mouth that you would have if you were going to whistle. (This is the equivalent of holding a straw – hence the name 'straw' breathing). It need only be a gentle position, not too forced, so that you can hold it for as long as you want.

Breathe in normally through your nose and let your breath fall out through your pursed lips. That is all you do! The action of letting the breath fall out, yet through a narrower aperture than usual, has the effect of lengthening and slowing the exhalation. Because this happens you will naturally take a slightly deeper breath when you next breathe in. You can continue in this vein for as long as you wish, making sure that there is no forced inhaling or exhaling, just a natural inbreath and a released outbreath.

If you wish, you can add to this routine, once you are completely comfortable with it, and deepen your breathing more. To do so, take a normal inbreath, but when you exhale through your pursed lips let the breath fall out for longer with each outbreath you make. Naturally your inbreath will be deeper too, but you do not need to make it so deliberately, just allow it to happen. Gradually you will get to the point where your lungs completely empty on the outbreath, and then the inbreath will be as deep as it can be. There may be a worry that you will not breathe in again if you let the breath out so far, but this will not happen – the inbreath cannot fail to happen because it is an instinctive action of the body. There may be a slight bump around the diaphragm area at the most empty point, and this will be the mechanism 'kicking in' to draw the air in again .

When you want to bring to an end any prolonged conscious breathing routine, all you need to do is to stop focusing on your breath. It will naturally be longer and deeper for a while after you stop. Just lie or sit still and relax until you feel ready to move. If you are lying down, roll onto your side to get up and push up from your side to a sitting position using your hands. Wait for a while, and then come up to standing.

Although the above description is of a routine which can be done whenever you have the time, or regularly once a day, you can use the basic way of breathing in through the nose and breathing out through the pursued lips at any time when you are feeling anxious or in need of calming down. Simply take a few conscious breaths in the way described, for as long as you feel you need, and allow the breathing to relax you, or bring you the space to be back in control.

White Eagle goes further: 'Having learnt on the physical plane to fill the lungs with fresh air and to exhale any poison, having learnt on the spiritual plane to inhale the spiritual sunlight as well, practise the inhaling through the right and left nostril alternately. There are two points in our being, the solar and lunar points of contact. The solar is made through the right nostril and you are breathing in to the solar centre; through the left, to the lunar centre. I think you do not need to go beyond this point at present.'

Circulating Life-Force:
A Meditative Exercise

Sit quietly and close your eyes, laying your hands palm upwards, one on each thigh.

Breathe gently and without effort, noticing the sensations as you breathe: the lungs pushing the ribs out at the sides; the coolness in the nostrils as you breathe in; the relaxing of the chest as you breathe out.

Imagine you are seated in a pool of light, which shines all around you, and even through you, like a magical but harmless ray in a science fiction story. This light is not only harmless, but full of health, well-being, comfort.

Focus on your breath again, and imagine that it is the means by which this light can flow into you. Imagine it flowing in through your left foot and left hand; travelling up through and around your head, and down and out through the right hand and foot. Be aware of this 'circulating light-stream' with every breath you take.

You don't have to breathe deeply, or change the rhythm of your breath at all; it simply happens, and will go on happening, even when your mind is elsewhere.

Feel that this 'stream of light' is being absorbed into every cell as you breathe in, and as you breathe out, it flows from you in a vibration of love towards all life.

After a few moments, take your thoughts away from your breathing, and become aware of the outer world again – your body on the chair, the sounds around you. When you open your eyes, wait for a while and know that this vivifying lifestream is constantly flowing in you; that your conscious awareness of it for this short while has cleared the channels and enhanced the flow of the Christ light. White Eagle says:

'Practise the method as follows. A good way to fall asleep is to lie on the left side with the left hand under the left cheek. This will automatically cause you to inhale more through the right nostril. You will help by putting the right hand under the left arm, because there is a nerve there which when pressed helps with this breathing. Sleep in this position and you will automatically be breathing in the solar energies, and thus inbreathing to your physical body and all the subtler bodies the aspiring atoms of life. It is these that we all need to attract and fill our beings with.'

7. Light in Meditation

LIGHT IS LIFE. And what gives that light its power and brings life to to all other things, both on Earth and in the universe, is spiritual light … the Christ light, as White Eagle has called it. The master Jesus said, *I am the Light of the world*.

Light is something which one becomes aware of in meditation, not only as light itself, but as love, because it is synonymous with the radiation of divine, unconditional love – the kind of love for humanity which Jesus demonstrated, a love which so transcends our conception of love that it is almost inconceivable. It is the love and life-force – the Light – which brought our Earth and the whole cosmos into being – the Light of God. The Christ Light not only gives life to all, but it is the life force which resides in the human heart.

'Your physical world is a world of illusion – it is not what you think it is. Do you realize that your physical world, in reality, is a world of light? It is built of light. Do you know that your physical body, if you could see it with clear vision, is composed of light? Only when you rise in consciousness in your meditations and aspirations to your Creator do you move into something which is adorable and lovely. Oh, the breath of the Infinite! The perfume of that breath! The joy of that life! Is it real, or is it something which will disappear in the morning? We answer that all that is holy, all that is pure and sweet and lovely is of God, and it is real. That is your real state of life.'

'The etheric body of a well-developed and evolved soul can be seen as being vibrant with light, as veritably sparkling – not merely with the magnetism of the physical body, but with life force, the light, which is contained in the etheric aura. If you could once realize that your body has a shield of light – if you could live always in consciousness of this light, you would find that the very atoms and the vibration of the atoms in your body would become etherealized. Then you would live for evermore in a body of light.'

'How dull, how depressed people feel without the sun! How joyous and happy they are when the sun again pours forth its light! Life then takes on a different complexion. Have you ever thought that you yourself are as a sun among the people with whom you mix; and that it is within your power to radiate sunshine and make happiness, just as much as it is within your power to withdraw the sun, and rob your companions of joy? Can we not each resolve henceforth to be a sun worshipper and a sunlight giver?'

'The sunlight which is reflected upon the earth (or appears to be thus reflected) is an outward symbol, on the physical body, through which the divine Life Force manifests.'

'What seems to be solid matter is not solid at all but full of divine energy and light.'

'May every day of life find you opening the windows, not only of your house but of your soul, to let the sunlight flood you. Sunlight you do not often see, you say; ah, there is invisible sunlight in the atmosphere! So when you 'open' you will grow in wellbeing, in the power to love, in kindliness to life. As the power grows more potent, so you will become more assured as to this invisible force, its reality and effect.'

Light

Wherever you are, let your eyes focus on whatever light there is as it is reflected off the objects and scenes around you. Notice the shadows created by the light, and the different qualities of that light. Is it a hard light, or a soft light? Is it subtle, producing less shadow, or clear and bright? How do different objects and the material they are made of reflect the light back to your eyes?

If you can, go into the natural world on a sunny day and look specifically at light there. As you will be aware, to look directly into the sun would be dangerous, but see how the sunlight is reflected in water, by grass, by clouds, off leaves and flowers. In particular, find the things which reflect the light the most, and break the light up into dancing particles before your eyes. See it on flowing, bubbling water, for example, or on shiny leaves when the wind is blowing, or long grasses in a field with the wind blowing across them, off rocks made of sparkling minerals, or see the light reflected by the rain.

Even in towns, you can find objects where light is reflected in scintillating ways. Feel the quality of light as it sparkles and shines, but also imagine that light shining from within the object, rather than just reflecting off it. For example, imagine light shining up from inside the water, or light shining through the petal of a flower from the inside. In both these cases it is not hard to imagine, since the petals and the water allow sunlight through them as well.

As you go about your daily life, be aware of light and how it affects you, the landscape and others. Stand outside on a dark night and be aware of the brilliance of the stars or moon, and reflect on the importance of light.

The more you focus on light in daily life, the more you are attuning your senses to it, and to its etheric counterpart.

Absorbing the Christ Light

In the following passages White Eagle helps us to understand the importance of light as something which we need to consciously take into our bodies. In meditation we are consciously attuning and absorbing this light through the heart chakra and thus affecting all the chakras and systems of the physical body. This in turn can bring about the healing he describes.

'Imagine a shining six-pointed star,* ablaze with light, and with a smaller white star in the centre, which is intended to illustrate the flow of the perfect, the Christ life, to men and women. We learn to absorb only the pure white light; and the colours visible in our aura and those of others are the individual vibrations resulting from absorbing the white light. Everyone must absorb a certain amount of the white light, else they could not live. Because so few absorb the full amount, few people are perfectly healthy and harmonious. Those absorbing only a tiny star of light find it insufficient to keep the spiritual and physical bodies harmoniously working. Therefore there are hold-ups at this chakra or that, which is the reason why we endeavour to heal through concentrating certain colours upon

*For the symbolism of the star, see p. 23 above.

certain centres.'

'Each main centre is attached to the spine – shall we liken the spine to the trunk of a tree, and the seven chakras to the branches? For down the spine are sensitive points at which the psychic centres are attached; for this reason manipulation of the spinal column is very helpful. Many healers concentrate upon the spine, with good reason. The life or spinal cord runs through the spine – but more, the vital centres of the body (beneath which are the ductless glands) are responsible for the health and wellbeing of the individual. If adequate supply of the divine life is carried into the body through correct breathing, physically, emotionally, mentally and spiritually, this spiritual food is circulated through the whole system.

'This white light can or should be absorbed through all these sensitive or power centres, but chiefly through the centre most harmonious to the Christ love – the heart. For you express Christ not through the mind only, although certainly the head and throat are brought into operation as well as the heart.'

Above the Clouds

If you have ever been in an airplane, you have probably experienced that moment when the plane rises up above the clouds, and you are in the sunlight again. Close your eyes and imagine that sensation of coming out above dark, heavy clouds into the light of the sun. Feel the lightness in as many ways as you can…

Feel the sun's rays penetrating every part of your body, the spiritual sunlight of God, as well as earthly warmth. Feel the relaxation of the body – letting tension dissipate, the muscles relaxing, and the smile of summer sunlight filling your heart and mind.

We can practise the ability to rise above the heaviness of earth into the sunlight, and sometimes repeating an affirmation can help. Choose one of those that follow, whichever fits you at the moment, and repeat it inwardly whenever you feel the need, remembering the warmth, lightness and light of the spiritual Sun, and the power of the Sun of God available within your heart.

- *I can rise above this; I can lift off like an airplane above all the heaviness of earth.*
- *I can get above the turbulent emotions and the worrying mind.*
- *I can find warmth, strength and peace above the mind and feelings.*

'Men and women have to find and establish in themselves a consciousness of the inner light. Once this inner light is recognized and gently encouraged to grow and develop, think, my brethren, what a difference it will make! If, instead of condemnation, argument and criticism, rash statements and hasty tempers; if, instead of these disturbing elements, gentleness, love and calm radiance shone through every man and woman, what a difference there would be!'

'It means that every individual striving to allow the great Light of the Christ to flow through them as they go about their business will radiate an influence which will be like the perfume of the rose, so powerful that their colleagues will feel the impact of that electric force. You do not know what electricity is – yet. We can tell you that this force we are describing is the Christ light; and that the radiation of spiritual thoughts is in a high degree identical with what is called electricity. You do not yet understand that the physical body and the etheric body which you possess is so related to the nervous system that it can animate and stimulate the psychic centres in the body. These centres become receptive to the eternal Sun – not the physical sun visible in the sky, but that power and light which is behind the sun. The nervous system of the body can become so sensitive and so attuned to the higher vibration that it can receive in great measure the electric power which has come from the inner sun, which is indeed the source of life.'

'My brethren, we want you to understand that spirituality is not something quiescent, but strong and powerful, finer than the matter of earth, finer than the earth vibration. It is the substance of its life. So it is true that as a man or woman becomes sensitive to the love of God, as they desire to become Christlike, so they bring through into physical life this power, this spiritual force. As they go about their business, other people feel this force in exactly the same way as you see a light which is switched on in a room. The person who has the inner light takes that light wherever he or she goes. Thus it is that the vibration of Christ sounds throughout the earth – it is the vibration of light, or of this highly refined electricity, and is felt and seen. People do not understand its nature, but they recognize that certain people seem to bring healing or a light as they enter a room. Those who recognize the light instantly acknowledge it. They bow in their souls, in their minds; they recognize something, they acknowledge it: the vibration of Christ, the Son.'

The Golden Light of the Spiritual Sun

Sit with your hands palms upwards in your lap and close your eyes. With each inbreath, imagine that every cell of the body, particularly in the upturned palms of the hands and the crown of the head, is taking in the light – in this case a warm, comforting, golden light.

There is no sense of strain. Just imagine that every part of you is like a magnet for that light to enter and flood the whole body with golden light.

And then with every outbreath, put your attention on the heart chakra at the centre of your chest and feel that golden light is radiating from there. As the breath goes out, the golden radiance spreads and fills the chest and gradually extends beyond it. Feel the spreading and opening of the physical chest, and imagine how at the etheric level that golden light is radiating in the expanding heart chakra.

Again, there is no strain to push out the light, or to think of where it might be going, just a focus on receiving light and then expanding in radiance.

So the limited mind is focused on breathing, on the surface of the skin, and then on the heart ... nothing more. The gold colour of the light brings warmth and strength, and also a feeling of safety, of being held in a much more powerful and reassuring protection than the mind of earth can provide.

'Having absorbed the white light, we use it in varying forms according to our degree of evolution, or according to the particular ray upon which we progress in the present incarnation. For instance, when the seventh predominates, we get mainly the violet colour in the aura. If the sixth, there will be a predomination of indigo. And so on, throughout the spectrum – according to our ray, so will that basic colour predominate. But do not forget this, that each colour has seven gradations or seven vibrations, indeed more.'

8. Still Mind, Open Heart

WHITE EAGLE says: 'The first necessity in your concentration is that of becoming still within, tranquil in heart.' These two states, stillness and tranquillity, encapsulate the state of meditation, the difficulties of meditating, and ultimately the aim of our meditation.

If we can find a still place in our minds, and a state of openness in our hearts or feelings, then we are in a good place to meditate. The very finding of both these states, however, causes many to give up, and to think that they can't do it. When we can touch the stillness of the mind and the openness of the heart, we realize that it is not only a means but an end in itself. It is as if the very stillness has a depth to it which transcends thought and even transcends mortality. The still mind is also like a lens to focus God's light on the bud of the heart to allow it to flower.

When we do reach the state of openness of heart, we find that God's love was always there for us within, and it is so profound and so far beyond earthly love that it conquers all that is not of itself. The comfort and transcending beauty of such a state is beyond description. The open heart is receptive, without guilt, innocent, accepting and joyous.

White Eagle was once asked, 'How can we best get in tune with the Infinite?' He replied, 'To still the mind is not easy. But when the simplicity and humility of love takes possession, then the spirit immediately becomes in tune with the Infinite.'

Focus on Stillness and Poise

What does it mean to be still? What if we were to say that stillness is not lack of movement, but something more like centredness? Could it be the kind of core stability from which we can move with grace, harmoniously, effectively and without losing our balance? Perhaps, then, an image to use would be the rod of light which is the inner spine. That's not something which is rigid – after all, the physical spine is curved and flexible – but which has a sense of strength, suppleness and centredness. From a core that is centred, one can choose to move, dance, laugh, flow, be spontaneous; when uncentred we know that we can be like a leaf on the surface of a river, at the mercy of the flow and without much choice as to where we will end up.

The Poise of a Dancer

When talking about stillness and poise it seems counterintuitive to mention dancing. However, the thing about training as a dancer is that one learns to develop an inner core which is so strong that when we move we do not lose our balance. This is poise, and it is one of those qualities which cultivating stillness brings for the meditation itself. It then becomes a trait that grows in oneself and which is of inestimable value in daily life.

Poise Creates Stillness

Thus we find that the qualities of centredness and poise help to enable our meditation. White Eagle describes their importance to our daily life when we are reaching for heaven:

'In the course of development the nervous system

becomes very sensitive, and you feel annoyance and irritation doubly – but that is all part of the training. You have to learn poise, which comes from the spirit.

'But as soon as you realize what is happening, stand upright with head erect, sending forth a thought to those spheres above the mists of earth, and you will receive through the head centre the baptism of the heavenly light and strength.'

The Spine as a Rod of Light

Sit upright, draw yourself erect and feel what happens within your body when you do this. The physical spine is curved, but the inner 'rod of light' of the spine, which is the linking channel of energy between all the chakras, is like a plumbline.

Drop your shoulders and feel as though the lobes of your ears droop too. Lift the heart and the crown, but without any physical lifting.

Use your will to visualize your inner spine as a rod of light which is balanced between heaven and earth, so it reaches right down into the earth through the hips and upwards beyond the crown of the head, with your self at the centre.

Now feel that you are drawing all your energies into the centre to be around the focus of the inner spine – to identify with the central poise of the spirit. It may be that you sense you are slightly off-centre in one part. Perhaps you sway very slightly this way and that, until your spine feels aligned with the spiritual forces. You may do this physically at first, but then imagine the inner adjustments and alignment which are happening. Keep focusing on this sense of getting closer and closer to perfect alignment.

As you do this, you will find you become more and more still and silent within; more and more lifted in all ways. Feel what happens, and the sensations which come to you. What you may enjoy is the true sense of poise. Recognize what it feels like. Become familiar with the sensation of poise and stillness.

Be aware of this feeling, trying to be completely still, and have the thought that just as your body and mind come into that poised space, so your aspirations can become lifted towards God – a sense of moving upwards without effort into the spiritual state.

You are linked with the spirit through this inner 'rod of light'; you are held safely and without effort in a state of poised receptivity. As you remain in this position, just being aware of this line of inner light, with all else dropping or relaxing away from it, so the inner will of your spirit takes over. You have created the conditions for this to happen and from here your meditation can unfold. However, even if you just stay with that feeling of deepest stillness and poise, you will find it is powerful in itself, as a means of bringing strength and the courage to will the will of God in your life.

The consciousness is already being raised, simply through this practice, which is one of the benefits of another spiritual technique, *zazen*, which is based on one of the great principles of life. It's a principle that White Eagle calls 'As above, so below'. Here we have the awareness that through the alignment of the physical body, we can also align to the spirit.

9. Why Stillness Works

WHEN WE MEDITATE, there is a reason for our trying to be physically still. It is that the nervous system that governs the muscles and tendons can then be in abeyance, and all consciousness can switch to the finer nervous system. This finer nervous system includes what White Eagle calls the 'etheric bridge' to the ethereal worlds and vibrations.

'You touch your chair; you feel with your physical body; and because you feel with the sense of touch, you think you are touching reality, forgetting that in a few years all these things return to nothingness. But what you are using on the inner planes, on the planes of spirit – these senses which you are creating and developing will live when all that is around you has passed and when the form that you know today is gone. The real things are those which come from your spirit, from your inner self, from the place of the "Knower": the "Knowing" within you.

'The "Knower" is the real, the true, the Higher Self. And the Higher Self knows Truth.'

In the passages in the next section, 'The Etheric Bridge', White Eagle begins by describing how we experience the world through our physical senses. He goes on to refer to senses we are using on the inner planes, which are the ones we are creating and developing in meditation.

When we are moving, we are employing our physical senses, often unconsciously, through the use of the physical nervous system. What we are seeking to do in meditation is to engage the finer nervous system, which is where being still becomes important. Stillness of body means that the muscles are not being stimulated, so the physical nervous system is not so engaged. As White Eagle says below, the finer nervous system, via the etheric body, is not something separate from the physical, but interpenetrates it. As the physical nervous system relaxes, so the etheric counterpart can take over. And as physical sensation shuts down, as the brain realizes that the body does not need to move, so finer, more subtle sensations can be realized and experienced. They come to the forefront of our awareness.

The Etheric Bridge

'The etheric interpenetrates the physical body and is connected to the nervous system. At death the etheric body is withdrawn and its lower part, being of the Earth, earthy, soon disintegrates. This important part forms the bridge between the finer worlds and the physical. Within this dense etheric body is also a finer etheric, which I will call the body of light or the vital body. This vital body again interpenetrates the lower etheric, and also interpenetrates the higher vehicles, the mental body, the intuitional body, and the celestial body. So we get a connecting link, a thread of light descending from the Christ sphere or plane of divine life, down through the various bodies into the etheric, the latter being the bridge which connects all to the physical sense or brain of a man or woman.'

'There exists a close relationship between the etheric body and the physical nervous system, and a continual exchange between the two. Now this exchange forms the link with the mind. So you will see that through the mind, through right thinking, harmonious thinking, you can send through your physical body an inexhaustible life force, because the mind centre is in direct contact with the life spirit, and the divine spirit.'

In the next selection of passages we will see how important it is to do all we can to create conditions which allow the 'etheric bridge', as White Eagle calls it, to be developed, if we wish to contact 'the different spheres or planes of spiritual life', to receive 'communication from the spirit spheres', to develop 'clear vision', to receive 'impressions' and to 'be receptive to the finer vibrations of life'.

'We find connection between the etheric body and certain centres in the physical body. Those of you who are students of medicine will recognize these centres as focal points of the main lifestream in the physical body which centres in the brain and spinal cord. These centres again are connected with the different spheres or planes of spiritual life.'

'This etheric body is an important part of your being; through this etheric counterpart of the physical, there travel the waves of light-vibration from the higher worlds of life; through the etheric body comes communication from the spirit spheres.'

'It is time to learn the secrets of the nervous system, for it is through the nervous system that the healing power flows to the healer; it is through the nervous system that inspiration comes to the individual; through the nervous system, clear vision and clairaudience is developed.'

'You do not yet understand that the physical body and the etheric body which you possess is so related to the nervous system that it can animate and stimulate the psychic centres in the body. All the psychic centres are connected with the endocrine and the nervous system, and it is through these centres and via the etheric body or soul body, that impressions come to the soul of man and woman from a life with which they are at present unfamiliar and in most cases quite ignorant of. We repeat that according to their sensitivity, so they may receive impressions via the soul or etheric body and nervous system, from a state of life which is not exactly outside the physical but is penetrating the physical life. For instance, if you are attuned to the soul life, you may receive, as you walk amid the beauties of nature at this time, impressions which will give you vision of the etheric world within the natural world.'

'The basis of all religion in the future is to be brotherhood of the spirit; and later, the development of a wonderful nervous system due to the quickening of the nerve centres of the body, so that human beings will be receptive to the finer vibrations of life.'

Awareness of the Bridge

Sit somewhere quietly and rest your hands in your lap. Look down at them and then watch them as you slowly raise them up and hold them out in front of you. Think of all the unseen processes in brain, nerves and muscles which have gone into you being able to do that. (If moving your hands is difficult, move any part of the body you can in the same mindful way).

Bring your hands back down for a while and then

once again raise them and extend the hands outwards. Imagine that your etheric body extends beyond the physical. Who would you like to reach in the world beyond this one? Imagine you are reaching across the bridge, and those in the world of spirit, perhaps your guide or loved one, or a dear animal friend, is stretching towards you.

You may not feel any sensation in your physical body, but you may feel the contact with them in your heart. Know that they are there, and, as White Eagle says: 'Where there is love, there is no separation'.

Safety

Stillness strengthens and widens that etheric bridge, so that the spiritual self can influence the physical. This means that all things can be felt more intensely: so that greater joy, passion and energy can arise. Far from being stifled or restricted, one can feel more alive.

However, in order to be still the body self has to feel safe. What is called the 'animal' or 'hind' brain needs to be sure that the body is safe. This is one reason why only positive thoughts of self and the process are going to help at this point. Any anxieties about oneself or one's abilities are going to be counterproductive, because the fight/flight, freeze/appease mechanism is still going to be active, ready to operate.

In chapter 10, 'What does it Feel Like?', we look further at the effects on the physical body of the finer nervous system being stimulated. Here we are looking at the feelings which arise in us as we reach that place of stillness. Not only do feelings arise but also qualities of consciousness which are developed in us for our soul growth and in order that we can live more harmoniously.

How to Create and Maintain Stillness

To create and maintain stillness, it is necessary to produce the most harmonious and comfortable conditions. This may mean sitting on a firm seat, with the spine as upright as possible; it may mean using as many cushions and supports as we need for the back, or if that is not possible, lying on a firm surface so that our muscles can relax. The point is to make the body so comfortable, without slouching, that we won't need to move.

Sometimes, however, no matter how well-prepared we are to begin with, we do need to move. On those occasions it makes sense, if our aim is to engage the nervous system as little as possible, to move slowly and quietly.… It really does make a difference.

Moving Slowly

Rest the backs of your hands in your lap, or beside you on the bed if you are lying down. Take three conscious breaths, one after another, and as you breathe in allow your hands very slowly to rise up; as you breathe out move them slowly back down. On the next three in-breaths, allow the hands to rise slowly upwards and outwards to the side; on the outbreaths let them come back slowly in and down to your lap. Feel the heart opening as the arms move out to the side.

If it feels comfortable to do so, continue repeating these very slow movements with the breath for as long as you wish, perhaps with the thought of being open and receptive to God's love.

White Eagle also links stillness with the silence. An exercise like the one we've just done, because of the increased awareness of how we are moving, can bring a degree of mental silence.

'What you can touch in the silence in your meditation lives for evermore. It means that a little more of your soul has been developed, has grown. It also means that an impression has been made upon those parts of your brain which before were dormant, but which now will gradually respond to divine truth.'

'My dear ones, enter the silence. Be still for a short time every day, morning and night. Surely God is worthy of a little attention in your busy life? Whenever you can withdraw from the crowd, seek contact with that divine life, which you will recognize in yourself as a vibration or feeling of peace, of love, and of great light.'

'The condition, then, for clear and perfect reception is one of stillness and silence, not only on the outer plane but deep, deep, deep within the inner world, the inner place. Underneath all conflicting vibrations, beloved ones, is the Silence. And in that Silence is God. God is behind all form, all activity, all manifestation. God is there.'

10. What does it Feel like?

MANY OF US would like to experience subtle energies in the same way as we do gravity or electricity, which are also invisible, but perceived by the body by the results of their action on matter. However, because subtle energies are subtle, their effect is often unrecognized. Therefore we remain unconscious of them. They are vibrations and affect matter as well, but we don't often recognize the signs.

Subtle energies cannot be felt in the midst of harsh, fast and loud movement, but stillness allows this recognition to take place. The brain, or the mind, learns what is important to us, in the same way that the other senses take over when one sense is lost – the other senses are enhanced to compensate without us deliberately doing anything. As we become still, the inner senses take over automatically.

It is a change in consciousness which is sometimes accompanied by an increased inner stillness. One analogy for the quality of that stillness is that it is like stepping out into a snowy landscape in which all sound is silenced.

The Thing about Subtle Energies is that they're Subtle!

It is hard to describe how it feels when you know you are touching the etheric level in a meditation. One way to describe it is just to say that you become aware, without an object to the awareness. It is an inner understanding which one cannot define or explain. As we saw earlier, White Eagle says one just knows, and that knowing comes from the higher self within always being in touch with the physical and influencing us, often without our awareness. So, when you meditate, you are reaching across that etheric bridge and the 'knowledge' from the greater part of your self is more accessible.

It is most definitely a feeling rather than a thinking process. White Eagle was once asked (making gestures which can be imagined from the words): 'Is there a simple way of meditation?' And he replied: 'The true way to meditate is first and foremost to withdraw from all earthly consciousness. Turn inwards and dwell upon the light of God which is deep, deep within our heart. Strive in that state to meditate upon love, compassion, tenderness, beauty – all the Godlike qualities of the soul. Dwell on that. Conceive the light that shines, focus on that glory which is deep, deep within the soul. From that point of light within the soul you will travel into realms of truth and beauty. Do not think here in the brain. Do not let your mind think. Contemplate here, in your heart.'

What qualities of feeling do we experience in heaven? White Eagle says spirituality has all the qualities of love, gentleness, kindness, peace, fearlessness, trust, joy, beauty, openheartedness, calmness, balance. But it also can manifest as a sense of poise, centredness, clarity and upliftment. It can feel as if the veil between the two worlds is falling away and understanding has arrived. Other sensations may be present-centredness, a wave of love, a feeling of connection, a release of tension, a sense of gratitude, a feeling of awe, timelessness or eternity, a sense of expansion, freedom, worship. The imagination can be stimulated, and sudden tears can come, along with a sense of divine flow, adoration, or greatly heightened sensitivity but with immense control and without excitement. There can be profundity, detachment, harmony, and a deep resonance within oneself. One can feel fearless, enjoy the infinite interdependence of all, and ultimately discover smiling bliss! In all these experiences, the consciousness is raised; the vibrations are being changed. These are also all aspects of the highest form of meditation (not lower mental or astral), which White Eagle teaches.

The Meditative Vibration

We can see from this list of its qualities that touching what could be called an exalted meditative vibration is not only linked with the higher vision or the hearing opening, but is also very much to do with feeling. As such, many of these subtle spiritual experiences can easily be passed over by the part of ourselves which might be looking for the grand moment, or expecting something more dramatic. It can also be seen that these fleeting awarenesses are not confined to meditation itself but can be experienced at other times.

Father Richard Rohr, a Christian contemplative in the Franciscan alternative orthodoxy, encourages us to be faithful to and to trust our own moments of contemplative experience, which is a perfect way to the spiritual unfoldment often talked about by White Eagle. In his work as a whole, Rohr identifies arenas in which these moments could occur, other than in meditation: prayer, nature, human intimacy, solitude, aesthetic experience, suffering, healing, philosophical reflection.

What we can do is to encourage ourselves to focus on these more subtle awarenesses when they arrive; to be prepared for them and to understand how easily they can pass. By doing so we can simply be with that moment, allowing ourselves the space to experience it fully, so that rather than trying to force it or ignoring it completely, the slight opening of the 'inner spirituality door' then has the opportunity to gradually widen. Through being aware at other times, when we come to meditate we have more chance to pick up on the subtle changes within us, the atmospheres and the feelings which arise from contact with the higher astral, mental and spiritual realms.

What Moments of Awareness Have you Had?

As you were reading the 'Meditative Vibration' passage it is quite likely that memories may have surfaced, maybe remembered within some of the arenas Rohr mentions.

Take each one of them, set out in the following list, and allow yourself to remember any spiritual, beautiful or loving awareness which comes back to you, giving thanks for them and allowing their vibrations, which remain in your aura, once again to permeate your conscious life:

- prayer
- nature
- human intimacy
- solitude
- aesthetic experience
- suffering

- healing
- philosophical reflection.

So meditation practice is not only a means to experience the spiritual while we are in physical form, but the feelings we experience point to a way of living which we are all working towards, unconsciously, while in matter. Those on a spiritual path are seeking to do so consciously. Meditation shows us the way. It shows us what it feels like to embody those higher sensations, to use the finer nervous system in harmony with the highest.

Although we have read some descriptions in this chapter, it is not easy to give names to the feelings that we experience through the finer nervous system when we are in a meditative state, because they are feelings which convey more than earthly words can contain. However, in order to make the feelings conscious, you may find it helpful to contemplate them so that they become marker posts to aim for. What follows is a list of a few of the feelings, or states of mind experienced in meditation, which you might spend some time contemplating:

For Contemplation

- *Poise* – a feeling of being completely centred and balanced, of being at the centre of one's true self where love, wisdom and power are not separate states but one ray of what one might call light.
- *Calm* – an awareness which is more than simple peace. It is the feeling that nothing can disturb you, no matter what happens.

- *Oneness* – this is the sense of not being separate from life at any level or from any form. It is a sense which takes away loneliness, and brings fellow-feeling at a deep level.
- *Fearlessness* – more than not being afraid, this is the sense that there is nothing to fear: that all is well and that God is in control inwardly and outwardly.
- *Clarity* – this is the feeling of being in a space which is uncluttered by the emotions and the disparities caused by separateness and the choices of the lower mind.
- *Knowing, awareness* – White Eagle calls the higher self the 'knower' within. This feeling is one of having a broader perspective which transforms the way we understand, and where all the senses act together.
- *Timelessness* – as one touches the higher planes of life, so the sense of time diminishes, so that a past life can go by in a flash of awareness and all that exists is the moment – now.
- *Joy* – happiness beyond earthly pleasure comes as one touches the plane of the 'knower'.
- *Tender-heartedness* – the ultimate and also the first feeling which is apparent; an overwhelming sense of gentleness towards all creatures and all people, which goes beyond any love we currently might know while in a physical form.

11. Experiencing Higher Vibrations

AS WELL AS the vibrations of light, all the vibrations of the Earth have their counterpart in spirit. Learning really to focus on earthly vibrations, we train ourselves to be more aware of those which are non-physical and subtle.

White Eagle says: 'Native American children were taught from childhood how to listen to the spirit world. In order to hear the voice from the world of spirit, they were taught first to listen to people on the earth plane, to give their whole attention to the one who was speaking to them. They were taught to listen also to the sounds of the birds and animals, the song of the wind in the trees, and the song of falling raindrops and the rushing river ... and because they were so trained, they were able to hear not only physical sounds, but sounds behind those of earth – the sounds of the unseen world.'

Beginning Really to Listen, to See and to be aware of Scent and Touch

Take a walk, sit, or lie outside, or with a window open, and listen to what you hear of the wind in the trees, or the birds.... This is sound vibration. Feel the music of the wind not only as something your brain interprets as sound, but as a vibration which passes through you and affects every particle of yourself. Imagine the cells of the body vibrating in and with the wind.

All life is vibration.

If there is no wind, look at the colours around you, and feel colour vibration, or take a few conscious breaths and be aware of the scents you notice. Again, be aware of these vibrations as not only sensed by the brain, but as the vibration which moves every cell, which influences your whole body and all your auras.

White Eagle once said in a service at his Lodge:

'Do you realize that some men and women have received more from the vibrations of the flowers upon the altar than from any word which has been spoken? It depends upon the particular ray upon which the individual vibrates. Some respond to vibrations of sound, some to music, some to perfume. Some respond to the vibrations of colour, so that colour in surroundings will affect these individuals while not affecting others. The vibrations, the harmonies of music, strike a certain centre in the soul, and cause it to open like a flower – to the sunlight, to the White Light of the Son, of the Christ, expressed by harmony.

'Through the sense of smell the angels or the dwellers in the land of light will convey their message to some; it is one of the methods used by certain masters to impress their presence, or ray, upon a pupil. Sometimes you may smell incense, and you say "Oh, this lovely scent of incense! I wonder where it comes from?" Actually you have received a ray from a wise one, and this is your particular way of reacting. Your conscious mind may not appreciate it, but the soul absorbs that vibration, that stimulation towards higher things. It may happen that a discarnate spirit discovers that your sense of smell has more acute responses than any other, and so brings to you a perfume which carries an association. Perhaps it is the scent of a hayfield, roses, violets, or the beautiful earth, wet with the gentle rain, or perhaps the scent of pines; these arouse in you a memory, and that memory will link you with your beloved.

'These things are not coincidence, but actually a law at work behind human life to impress upon the soul conditions not limited by time or matter. Through these higher senses, the soul of a person is released into the land of light. As you realize these vibrations in your life, so will you become more attuned, more awakened, more aware of the real life, the eternal, the life of the spirit.'

'There is no short cut to true seership. You who desire to develop clairvoyance should commence by being very observant. Train your vision: always, everywhere. Try to understand what is behind form, and visualize the emanations from form, and in that way you will gradually develop the gift of true seership.'

'The ancients worked upon the plan in human life, for they knew that as below on earth, so above in heaven. This was one reason why the Sages taught their pupils to be very observant about life, and why the simplest human experience is so important, because it reveals to the wise a divine principle.'

'In the mystery schools and training schools of the past as well as in the temples of training in the spirit spheres, the teachers concentrated for a long time upon helping their pupils to use their observation and to control their thoughts and emotions.'

Encouraging Sensory Awareness

The sections on each of the five senses that begin on p. 77 are designed to help us observe – in the way that Native American children were taught to do, and how those in the mystery schools of the past were encouraged. In these sections we learn not only to observe and therefore develop the sense of sight, but discover ways to stimulate all the physical senses; and because of the principle, 'as above, so below' the higher senses used in meditation are developed in the process.

Observing

Read again one of the passages from White Eagle above, and bring your attention to how these words resonate within you, how you feel, also to where you are and what is around you. Really observe the moment in all its detail – not by concentrating more, but by simply seeing and experiencing it, with a calm, detached view.

What do you notice within yourself? Instead of intellectualizing the words you have read, feel their impact upon you – allow the sense of the words to become part of your consciousness. The mind registers and makes sense of what the brain has received, a fraction of a second later. Give yourself time to absorb what you have read before moving on. This doesn't mean you have to read every sentence ponderously. Rather, read a whole section, but then feel your response within before moving on to the next.

> What you are doing is learning to live in the moment, rather than only live in your thoughts. Instead of swimming frantically on the surface of life, you are allowing yourself to float calmly on the surface, and to explore what lies beneath. You are allowing the flashes of intuition time and space to arise from within.

Expanding the Consciousness through Expanding the Senses

'It is very important that all of you understand the value of form, because it is form through which the spirit manifests. Not only physical form: there is the form of beauty in nature. Through beauty in nature you glimpse the divine spirit, this radiance, this love. Through the grandeur of nature, you glimpse the power of that spirit, and likewise through the harmony of music, which is another form on the earth or in the heavens. It is a form, a sound-form through which the Creator manifests.

'As you wander in the woods, in a temple or gardens, as you inhale the perfume of the rose, through that perfume you make contact with your Creator, with God. And when you taste pure food, pure and beautiful fruits, when you taste the crystal water of the spring which falls from the hillside, you are tasting the form in the water of the Creator, God.

Developing the Senses of the Soul

'Through all your senses of vision, of taste, of hearing, of inhaling the air and perfume, and of touching beauty, you are using all your senses to make contact with the Divine Creator, with God, your Father–Mother.'

In order to encourage awareness through the senses, in each of the following meditations we focus on one physical sense at the beginning, which then leads us deeper into the awareness of the etheric counterpart in the meditation.

Sight

Gaze at something that is uplifting in its beauty. It may be a picture, a candle flame, the sky, a flower or tree from your window – something which makes you feel good about life, and which brings the vibration of beauty or poise. Already, as you do this, you are raising your vibration, though you may not be aware that you are.

As you close your eyes, carry that image with you into your inner world. Imagine it there, and then see it even more radiant, irradiated with God light, and giving off a vibration or perfume of loveliness, an essence of divine love.

Whatever the image you take into your meditation, now let it expand. If it is a flower, for example, imagine in what place the flower is growing at this inner level. If it is a scene from a picture, imagine the scene filling with other things: people, animals, more natural beauty. If it is a flame, imagine what kind of sanctuary that flame would be placed in.

As you focus on beauty, so the angels will draw close, and you may be able to imagine their presence in that exquisiteness of the inner world.

It is important that you keep the idea in your mind that your consciousness is being raised, and that all that you will see is of a God-like essence or quality. This will keep your consciousness lifted above the astral and in the more spiritual realms.

Sound

Before you enter meditation, listen to uplifting sounds: some music which lifts your heart, but is not too dramatic, loud or fast; or to the song of the birds outside your window, or to a Tibetan bowl or cymbals, if you have them. Indeed, if you play a musical instrument of any kind (no matter how much of a learner you are!) you could play something simple and melodious on it. Alternatively, you could sing or chant, with the idea that it is preparation for your meditation.

As you play, sing or listen, imagine that sound coming to you from the inner worlds, or being stimulated by your spirit. With such a thought in mind, your consciousness will be raised.

Close your eyes when the music ends, and see if you can imagine the sound still coming to you. Follow the sound into your higher consciousness, imagining it sweeter, richer, more harmonious than the sounds of Earth. Go towards it, and feel that it grows in depth and gives off a vibration of harmony, of love, as it does so.

Allow yourself to imagine where that sound is coming from in the world of spirit. For example, if you have been listening to voices, or chanting, it may be that you begin to see monks or a spiritual choir, or your higher self. If you have been playing an instrument, perhaps you will see the heavenly orchestra, the healing temple where such music is used, or find that the angels of music are close, and you can imagine their joy and begin to hear 'the music of the spheres'. If you have been playing a Tibetan bowl, sometimes it can feel as if you find yourself inside the sound, as if you are inside a bowl of light, with the spiritual essence of that sound penetrating and healing every part of you.

Touch

For the beginning of this meditation, it is helpful to take your awareness into your body. One way is to be consciously aware from the start of how you are sitting on your chair, and how your feet are placed on the floor. Feel the support of the floor and the chair – the firmness or otherwise – and how your hands are placed in your lap. Feel the texture of the material of your clothes under your hands and the warmth or otherwise of your skin – how the air feels against your hands and face. Feel also inside your body – the sensation of breathing in your chest, how your stomach feels and your head. Be aware of the relaxation or tension around your eyes and on your brow and make a conscious decision to let go.

This kind of body awareness can bring you out of the busy-ness of the mind, and make you more aware of the sensations you are experiencing – and, since it is the mind that tends to inhibit us and bring tension and activity, focusing on the body can bring us to a place of stillness within, which is indicative of the consciousness being raised.

As you are aware of the sensation of air against the skin, and the touch of material, imagine what it would be like to extend your hands into the inner world. What would you be able to touch there?

Gradually allow this awareness of an inner sense of touch to grow. For example, if you have a loved one in spirit, imagine holding their hand, or feel the touch of their hand on your shoulder. If you love water, imagine the joy of swimming without fear in a beautiful lake or sea of blue, where the water feels healing and buoys you up, not only physically but spiritually. If you love the earth world, imagine standing against a tall tree, feeling the strength of its trunk, or sitting on warm rock overlooking a beautiful valley, breathing in the sweet, clear air of the mountains.

Another way to enter a meditation based on touch is to do a walking meditation beforehand. In this you practise the same degree of focus and awareness as above, but while walking slowly, and ideally in natural surroundings – maybe even barefoot. This can form the basis of the whole meditation in itself, where your awareness becomes heightened to a fine degree by every sensation of movement, of the air against the skin, of how the ground feels, and by experiencing touching the growth around you and feeling the contours of the earth.

Smell

Begin your meditation by focusing on breathing. Don't try to change your breath, but just be aware of how you breathe and feel the sensation in your nose and the back of your mouth as you breathe gently in and out. You may then like to inhale the perfume of essential oils which are uplifting and calming, or of your favourite flowers. Or, as you are gently breathing, you may like to remember what the scents are that you love – perhaps the vibrancy of new-mown grass or hay, the salty tang of the sea, the sweetness of certain flowers, the pungency of the air in a wood of pine or fir, the aroma of earth warming up after winter. Imagine breathing in these scents now.

It may be possible for you to walk or sit in the natural world and inhale the scents described above. If so, then allow the air to bring to you what it will. As you breathe, see if you can experience more than the scents, maybe the deeper connection between all life. As you breathe in that air with such a deep awareness, as White Eagle says, the angels of light are drawn close to you.

When you sit to meditate, imagine those scents you have experienced as particular vibrations. Allow each scent you think of to speak to you of a soul quality which it brings. Expand your awareness to imagining where the perfume is coming from. For example, if it is a flower perfume, where is the flower growing? If it is the sea, what does it look like and how is the scent of the sea reaching you? If it is a wood, imagine you are walking there.

As your consciousness is raised, on the wings of the angels of light, feel that you are being surrounded by that perfume, and can experience with your whole being the soul quality of that perfume permeating every cell of your being at that inner level.

Taste

'We relate the element water to the sense of taste. That may sound perplexing to you, but let the inner self speak. For instance – drink the water from a running brook, drink the sparkle and the sunlight which gives it life. Do you taste water only? No, more than water, an indefinable, indestructible element – you drink the very life of the Earth, take in a very part of the cosmic body, the life force. Through the sense of taste which we relate to the water element, you can create or bring about in your physical body the turbulence of a storm, or surpassing harmony and peace. Think well on this. Through the mouth harmony and peace can enter – or tempest, creating havoc in the physical body, like that in the ocean.'

'The sense of taste within will bring harmony, will create peace and a well-ordered microcosm. Or it will do the reverse.'

To prepare for this meditation, you may like to eat or sip something with as much awareness as you can for its flavour and texture. Grannies used to tell us to chew our food well, and maybe this is an opportunity to do just this, and also to give thanks as you do so for the fact that you have enough to eat, and for the abundance that Mother Earth supplies. As you eat, imagine not only that this food is becoming part of your physical form, but that it contains spiritual energy, the light of the Sun, both physical and spiritual, which brings vitality to your being. Feel that you can be aware of your body being strengthened and renewed by this food and revitalized by this drink.

When you shut your eyes for meditation, imagine yourself with gratitude picking a fruit from a beautiful tree in an orchard or hedgerow in the world of spirit. See the fruit filled with divine light, and as you bite into it, imagine that divine light not only filling you, but raising your consciousness upwards. As you expand in awareness, visualize yourself in your own special sanctuary in the world of light – a place which is special to you, and which is just as you would like it to be.

In this sanctuary the Master has prepared a table for you with the bread and the wine – the essence of spiritual life and light. Imagine yourself receiving this communion from the Master and explore the taste of the bread and the wine from the grail cup, as they are passed to you by the Master's hands.

As before, feel that you are consuming and making your sustenance not just physical substance, but the substance of God. You may even be aware of the angels of ritual gathered to assist.

Feeling and Awareness with all the Senses

Besides the sense of physical touch there is also the sense of feeling – not emotion, as on Earth, but a deep, inner awareness of love, peace, beauty, strength, wisdom, joy.

To begin this meditation, it is helpful to think of someone or something we love, or of a place where one has felt deep peace and stillness. We allow the feeling of earthly love or peace to wash through us. We feel the change that happens to our face, and the tension in our body relaxes, as we love.

Feeling

As you enter meditation, imagine a love reaching out to you which is infinitely greater than that which you have felt – a love without judgment or limitation. Feel yourself loved, comforted and uplifted. This love is so powerful it can lift you beyond the fears and limitations of your earthly body and mind. Indeed, at this moment your angel will be surrounding you with an aura so connected to spiritual love that you will be raised in consciousness, whether you are aware of it or not. Love is so potent it draws love to itself.

Expanding your awareness, imagine the world of spirit where all is love, beauty, peace, strength, understanding and joy. Your guide or master will be there for you if you wish, but it does not matter if you cannot see them, or your vision is hazy or only comes in flashes. In this meditation it is all about exploring the spiritual feeling of your unlimited, spiritual self. Whatever feeling you need, allow yourself to experience it. Imagine yourself being enfolded in it; or that feeling being radiated to you by your guide. What would make you feel most loved, most at peace, most strong? What would lift your heart with its beauty or joy? What would most bring you understanding? Whatever your answer it will be there for you – flowing to you.

There can also come a point in meditation when all the senses become one, when we are simply profoundly aware at the spiritual level – and it feels as if all the impressions of the senses have come together in this overriding awareness of spirituality, spiritual contact, of beingness – of being spiritual.

12. Reaching for the Highest

PEOPLE OFTEN ask what the difference is between visualization and meditation. In one sense the one simply includes the other, in that meditation in the way taught by White Eagle often uses visualization and imagination. To answer this question more completely, though, we need to think in terms of levels of consciousness, or in old-fashioned terms, planes of consciousness, such as those described by Sir Arthur Conan Doyle in ARTHUR CONAN DOYLE'S BOOK OF THE BEYOND.[1]

White Eagle talks about rising in consciousness through the astral and lower mental, to contact the higher realms. When we do so he likens it to 'entering the temple of the spirit', which is both individual and universal.

'We know that many of you, during your meditation, have been able to enter the temple of the universal brotherhood. But how many have seen the canopy or roof of that temple, which is formed of the protecting love of the Creator? You will have seen that it is supported by pillars. Yes, these pillars, which support this canopy of protection, are the qualities of the soul. If you will think this out, you will clearly understand what is meant. You pray, you sometimes cry out in your need to your Protector, the Great White Spirit; but in order for you to receive full protection you need to develop within yourselves qualities of the spirit which are like the pillars supporting the

*Liss, Hampshire (White Eagle Publishing Trust), 1994, 2003

canopy. This means that when in daily life these Christ-like qualities are put into operation by spiritual law, all the protection, the guidance, the help that a soul needs comes to them.

'We would have you know that the descriptions which are given to you of the spirit temple, the temple gardens, the homes of the people in the invisible world, the temples of learning, the temples of wisdom, the temples of art and science, are of real places; they do not exist only in imagination – they are real, enduring structures.'

There are many ways to daydream, to visualize and to use the imagination, and for a number of different purposes. Some are to create, to draw things to oneself and to worry about what could happen or reflect on what is gone. In these cases, one is tapping into a level of consciousness very much associated with the Earth, and therefore with limited understanding. But the use of the imagination in meditation takes us beyond all of this; quite simply, we move into realms of consciousness which are more spiritual, in the sense of their being associated with unconditional love. We do this through making a deliberate focus, at the beginning, on God, the light, the star; in other words on the highest spiritual form we can in that moment conceive. This, White Eagle says, lifts the mind and feelings beyond the earthbound state where all kinds of negative influences can intrude. Many, following the White Eagle meditation, have experienced this. White Eagle describes it here as rising up to the apex of the triangle.

'In your meditation we direct you first of all to go right up to the apex of the golden triangle and there meditate upon the Great White Light or the Golden One, the

Christos, the Supreme Light. As you do this, as you go directly and earnestly to that point and as you focus your worship, your adoration, your consciousness in that universal and infinite Light, you must also at the same time use all your chakras. In other words, you must bring all your devotion, all your power to that one supreme point. This creates in you the perfectly straight line of light which comes from the base of your body or the kundalini right up through the spine to the crown of the head. It is just like the plumbline which the mason or the builder uses. This is the meaning of the plumbline. Not only is your body straight, and the power rising straight up through your body, but all your concentration is on God, on what is good, what is lovely, what is beautiful, what is true, just and wise; the whole being is brought into poise, into straightness.'

'True imagination comes as the result of the reaction on the brain of higher vibrations which have been set in motion by your sincere aspiration and prayer. You can think all kinds of unworthy and foolish thoughts with your lower mind, but when you have touched that power and light then you are suffused with God power, and that affects not only your higher mind but your brain. Thus you are able to create, by the power of God, the form described to you to help you to break through into the world of spirit.

'This is why we always guide you first of all to go right up to the highest heights, to the great white and golden spirit, and there make your contact. Once you have made that contact, you can give yourself to the unfolding vision, which will carry you on beyond your leader's guidance.'

Creating a Starting Point

One way to reach for the highest is to have a starting point for your meditation which is a focal point for your awareness. The passages in White Eagle's book THE STILL VOICE,* for example, often have one simple image such as a still white flame, or a rose opening in the light of the sun, as their starting point.

Focusing on such an image helps the mind, body and emotions to be brought to a point of stillness and poise. All the focal points in the list below are taken from White Eagle's teaching and deliberately invoke a particular spiritual vibration. They lift the consciousness to a higher plane and resonate with the highest within the meditator, albeit subtly and often unconsciously:

- A crystal, possibly one in the heart of a lotus.
- A still flame.
- A fragrant rose.
- A lotus unfolding on the surface of the water.
- The still surface of a pool reflecting the light of the sun.
- The six-pointed star.
- A sphere of light at the heart centre, expanding outwards.
- A golden pyramid of light representing the apex of a mountain.

Choose one of these images to work with for a while, beginning your meditation with a deliberate creation of the image itself, but more importantly allowing the

*Liss, Hampshire (White Eagle Publishing Trust), 1981, 2006

vibration of the image to stir your feeling nature. For instance, what feeling does the fragrance of a rose generate within you? What feeling does expanding light in your heart give you?

In this way you move beyond trying to see something that may be fleeting and incomplete and aim to embrace the spiritual response the image is designed to stimulate within you.

13. Creating and Becoming Aware at Levels beyond the Physical

THERE ARE a number of questions that are frequently asked in the teaching of meditation the White Eagle way, and many of them centre around the use of the imagination, and what is and is not real. For example, students are concerned whether they will be able to 'see' in meditation, and often in a led meditation, and people ask if they should always follow the leader's guidance, or whether they should follow what comes to them individually.

The first thing to remember is that when White Eagle is talking about the imagination, he is not just referring to seeing but, as set out in previous chapters, the use of all the senses, including the ability simply to sense overall: to be aware, to feel. So although the two stages below relate to visualizing, this implies the use of all the senses, and the stages outlined can be sequential, but are not always.

Two Stages of Visualization

The first stage in visualization is what one might call 'creating in the ether', which simply means using our imagination to create something mentally, but at a higher level than just visualizing. White Eagle makes this clear by referring here to our aspiration and the use of the higher will of God. The use of the starting, focal points mentioned in the previous chapter would be one way in which one is creating in this way.

'Through aspiration and the will of God at work within, you create your inner world, your temple. We would point out that those things that you see in meditation are not deception. They are real places created by the aspirant. By soul-effort the aspirant is building the temple he or she beholds.'

The second is when we become aware of things at an etheric, or spiritual level, which we have not deliberately set out to create. In other words, we begin to see or experience something which exists at the etheric level. Perhaps it has been created by us in other lives, and still exists at this soul level. Perhaps it has been created by others, and comes to us in order to teach, to inspire, to comfort and to release.

For instance, what makes one person think of a white lotus, rather than a golden one? What makes this person feel a sense of strength, when others think peace? What makes yet another find themselves walking up the steps of an Egyptian-style temple, when the leader was seeing a Christian church? What brings to a person the sudden smell of warm stone? What causes someone's grandfather suddenly to appear in their mind's eye? What makes a person hear the sound of bells or the sea, or the wind or the birds? There are many times in meditation, for example, when things happen which a meditator would not normally have chosen – not unpleasant things, but places, for example, that they would not automatically have visited, people they would not automatically think of seeing, or sounds and visions which are outside even a fantasy world.

To recap: in meditation we may start off with something we deliberately choose to 'see', but it can evolve, and then other things are experienced which we have not deliberately chosen. No matter how unexpected this is, there is naturally a tendency to be wary; to be concerned that this second stage of becoming aware at an inner level is just associative, or self-created. In one sense, of course, it is self-created, by the greater self, but how do we know it is not associative – the mind going from one thing to another as in word associations? Sometimes it will be, and sometimes we are fortunate enough to have evidence that this cannot be so. One such example, under the heading 'The Blue Topaz', is given at the end of the chapter.

As we continue to meditate, more and more such evidence comes to the fore. However, something deeper and more lasting happens as well. There emerges the kind of evidence which is not provable in earthly terms, but is a complete inner knowing that we are in touch with something other than the earthly conditions. This kind of deep conviction can sometimes last for a long time, and sometimes not, depending on a person's life – White Eagle says that 'the graph of the spiritual path goes up and down'. There are times when we are simply testing our faith, or our endurance.

And sometimes, particularly at the outset, we have to go through the creating stage before we become aware. But sometimes the conditions within ourselves are so right or powerful that suddenly our inner eyes and other senses are open, without the need to create.

'It should be remembered that the first step towards meditation is sincere worship of and devotion to the Great White Light, because this particular method of meditation is designed to encourage the growth and expansion of the Christ Light in the human heart. During meditation, persevere with the practice of dwelling on the enfolding love of the spirit of Christ. Search for that spark of light within yourself, for this will surely shine amidst the darkness. If necessary, use your power of imagery in order to create this light in your consciousness. See it shine out like a jewel, like a diamond glistening and pulsating with lovely colour and radiance.

'If and when you can do this, remember it is only the beginning of the real awakening and development of your spiritual vision or clairvoyance. Accept this light as your starting point. Then, as development proceeds, its gleam will grow larger and brighter, and presently expand to a sun-like disc, looking very bright and beautiful. Remember that all this will take place within yourself and is to be seen subjectively but not objectively – within your inner vision but not with your physical eyes. The next phase will be to project yourself into and through this disc of light and then (still using your gift of imagery or spiritual imagination) to visualize yourself as entering into another world, a new world created out of finer ether, which is itself a kind of rarefied light.'

The Blue Topaz

This evidential story comes as an example from someone who has practised meditation in the White Eagle way for some time: 'Many years ago, during meditation, I found myself in a crystal temple in the world of spirit. In the central area a huge crystal was suspended from above, and around the room were smaller chapels. Each had their own different crystal. I was drawn to one and spent some time contemplating a beautiful pale blue crystal, which gave the vibration of gentleness and calm sweetness. I did not recognize the crystal, but heard the word 'topaz'. With that part of my mind still attached to physical life I dismissed this, since to my earthly mind topaz was gold. Imagine my delight when several weeks later, whilst flicking through a coffee table book on crystalline rocks, I recognized the precise blue of my meditation crystal and saw the words 'Blue topaz from the Ural mountains in Russia'. This happened long before they became common stones for jewellery in this country.

Painting with the Mind

Sit or lie comfortably. You are an artist, able to work in more than three dimensions; able to create anything from any angle you wish.

This time create a still pool in front of you – blue, clear, shining. Go down under the water, in your imagination, and create a lotus bud resting in the mud. Draw it with your mind – a bud on a stem, which you lengthen upwards towards the surface of the water. Extend the stem, waving slightly up until the tip of the lotus bud touches the surface. In your mental picture sketch in the slight ripple as it breaks the surface.

Time elapses, and now you draw the stem as it reaches up, in the light of the sun, and you create the bud beginning to open. You may find you draw the leaves spreading out on the surface – with their lovely curving shapes – and then focus again on drawing the lotus petals opening, until you create the open flower, cupping the stamens. Lotuses can be many different colours. Paint yours to suit your mood, including the colour of the centre.

Why stop there?! Create the perfume of the lotus. Create the smoothness of the petals. Create the feeling you receive as you gaze at its heart.

14.
Don't Expect it to Be the Same: the Practice of 'Desirelessness'

ONE OF THE distinguishing characteristics of being in a human body is that we have the ability to look backwards and remember, as well as to look forwards and anticipate. These may both be joys but they are not generally useful when we come to meditate.

'The first object of your meditation must be love, God, the Source of your being.… It is necessary for you to have an objective – not in your head chakra, but in your heart – which is born of selfless love. Therefore the first requisite for meditation is selflessness or, as some would say, 'desirelessness'. We prefer the term 'selflessness'. The pupil should not desire anything that will enhance his own powers nor glorify himself. He has one object – adoration of the Beloved – seeking to draw close to the Beloved. What is the Beloved? The Beloved is life, universal life: spiritual life, which has many forms through which it manifests. The would-be meditator learns in the practice of meditation to become at one with universal life. It is, as our eastern teachers tell us, the act of the dewdrop merging into the ocean.'

To desire is not just about acquiring things, of course, but also about wishing to repeat experiences or have special ones. In meditation we might be desirous when we have expectations that things will happen, be the same, be more obvious, and so on, coupled with the expectations we have of ourselves.

We would suggest that to practise desirelessness, as White Eagle describes it, is to go into the meditation with no expectations that anything will be the same as before. This does not mean that we can't develop certain rituals, like beginning the meditation in the same way each time, but if we stick too rigidly to them and expect everything to work as it has done previously, then we limit ourselves and the opportunity for our creative intuition and imagination to work, besides running the risk of becoming frustrated when things are different and what we expected does not happen.

At the same time as not desiring anything of the meditation, expectations of the self as a meditator can also produce frustration when we don't seem able to do it. Why do people give up on something? Sometimes, perhaps, because they feel they can't do it and they want to be able to. That is a desire. What if there was nothing that one had to get right; no unalterable aim, no desire to be desired, just a beingness?

In the next passage, White Eagle seems to be demonstrating the value of meditation in daily life, even though one is simply 'being'. By the same token, taking away the desire to get the technique right or to recreate the same conditions as before can inhibit the ability to be simply God-conscious.

'Meditation and union with God is of the utmost value in daily life. It is better to be good than to dissipate energy in an endeavour to do good. Being good, being God-conscious, being God-loving, being God-wise, does far more to help life than misplaced energy which is trying to do good. Therefore choose being, rather than seeming to be.'

A Variety of Meditative Experiences

It is thus important to let go and not expect to recreate the same meditative experience each time, knowing that the ability to meditate can vary from day to day, or from time to time. It is helpful, therefore, to know that in meditation it is possible to have different kinds of experience, which will depend on our need at the time, the needs of our greater self, or guidance. These categories may be loosely described as:

•   A teaching meditation – where we feel we receive some kind of deeper understanding.

•   A silent meditation – where the meditation does not greatly involve the inner senses, but instead a profound stillness, an awareness of God at a deep level in the silence.

•   A creative meditation – in which we are particularly aware of unfolding or renewing, or transformation.

•   A past-life-oriented meditation – when we experience or are aware of an earlier incarnation.

•   A healing meditation – in which healing or a special blessing comes to us.

•   A sensory meditation – in which the inner senses are being developed through experiences in the spiritual life.

•   Meditations that invoke particular seasons and festivals/phases of the moon/solar events such as equinoxes.

As can be seen, it is possible to experience a variety of meditations using the same method. Not every meditation has to be the same. It is also possible for a single meditation to fit more than one of the categories given.

Wuwei – Effortless Effort

Another way to think of this idea of 'desirelessness', and more importantly to practise it, is to be found in what White Eagle calls 'going with the tide': 'You get set ideas as to what you want and what you think we want, which are not always right, you know. We say to you, go step by step and take whatever path is open to you. Think well, accept and trust. One step leads to another. Let your minds be malleable. Remember that in the world of spirit the condition of life is not rigid, it is fluid, it is moving all the time, moving forwards to harmonious and beautiful states. Just go with the tide.'

'Going with the tide' is analogous to the Taoist term *wuwei*, which loosely translates as the anomalous phrase 'effortless effort'. Yet that is the exact something which meditation requires. Making a true contact can be undermined by too much effort of the forceful kind. Rather, it is an immersion in something; a letting go into God, as you will read in the next chapter on 'Resting'. What a relief it would be to just sit or lie and let go into God!

White Eagle describes why this letting go works in this way: 'If you are sorely troubled, remember there was a time before you became a separate entity in a physical world, when you were at one with your Creator on that beautiful level of life in the heaven world.

'There you were at one. Down here you are separate. But if you can rise in consciousness and put yourself in tune with the Infinite, you will see your problems and difficulties from a very different angle. You will know that all things work together for good, for God, for those who love God. Surrender then will be so simple. All the fret and the fear will all fall away.'

The Secret and the Power of
Letting Go and Letting God

Imagine as you sit, ready to meditate, that you could hear God, or a master, saying to you: 'Let go and let me take care of it all'. And for all you know he means not just taking care of your life and health, but that of your friends, the animal kingdom, other peoples and the world. In fact, all the things you are anxious about; all the things which make you tense or angry or around which you feel powerless.

Just imagine it now. Close your eyes and feel the presence with you, the presence which can do anything, and which knows everything and how everything fits together in the grand scheme and throughout time. Feel that that presence also knows every hair of your head and therefore you have nothing to be anxious about, even when it seems you should worry from an earthly perspective. All is taken care of and all will be well. So even if you can't quite believe it, imagine how it might feel to hear those words, feel that reassurance, that support, care and underlying strength.

Now feel how your shoulders relax, your eyes relax, you find you take a deeper breath on a sigh of release – and you surrender into that care. That is the beginning of your meditation.

Whenever you feel agitated, or not getting there during the meditation, come back to that thought and feeling; if you manage just that, you will be healing every part of yourself, as well as raising your vibrations.

Surrendering and Grace

As we have just seen, part of the process of meditation is in the act of surrender. Even the act of taking time out of daily life to meditate is an act of surrender – of surrendering the busy-ness and outward concerns of life to the inner world of spirit, to the higher consciousness.

Then comes the surrendering of the mind and of any feelings which may be getting in the way of making a spiritual contact. This can be a process of struggle or, instead, of slipping into a familiar and comforting state. If we struggle, then the vibration cannot be raised so easily. If we consciously and willingly surrender, then it is easier.

What is more, when we consciously surrender then we receive what has been called divine grace – the inner world becomes more real and present for us. In that act of surrender we align ourselves with the greatest spiritual understanding and power, and thereby open ourselves to its magic. White Eagle has said, at a festival time:

'Here then is the picture, the story of Eastertide. Try to relate this to your own lives and see in that symbolism a truth which will fill you with joy. It points not to death but to life, but it must be by the way of surrender.'

'This is what we mean when we point to the Cross of Light. For the soul who would receive that cross, who would bear that cross within his or her heart, must have learnt the lesson of discrimination and surrender ... surrender of the lower self to the Divine. So you see what the surrender means ... what the sacrifice of the cross means? It is not easy. It sounds easy perhaps, looks easy on paper; but when it comes to putting it into action in everyday life, it is one of the hardest lessons that human beings have to learn.'

'In this symbol of the cross within the circle with the Star at its heart, we have a representation of wisdom and love combined, which is to be realized by humanity in this new age.'

Surrender and Grace: a Process of Practising Surrender in Preparation for Meditation

Think of something in yourself that you wish to surrender. You may wish to surrender to something which is happening in your life, or to surrender something – even a habit.

Picture the cross within the circle: another thing White Eagle has said is that 'the symbol of that ray of light which inspired St John is the equal-sided cross within the circle – the symbol of' of the self into the circle of eternal love, which alone brings true wisdom.' Imagine yourself at the heart of that cross, placing yourself or whatever you wish to surrender there.

Now see that there is a star of divine grace at the heart of the cross within the circle, and imagine what would flow back to you, from that star, as a result of this surrender (this will be different for each person – it may be a quality, an opportunity, or a different relationship with someone or something).

Accept this grace by being as you imagine you would be as a result of receiving this, even if it does not immediately appear to be happening outwardly. Remember, things happen etherically before they happen physically, and take time to work through to the outer awareness.

The ultimate act of surrender is something which the Master Jesus demonstrated, and which White Eagle refers to as the earth initiation: 'The crucifixion has an even deeper meeting which applies to you, for it is indicative of the last of the four great initiations which every human soul must undergo on its journey back to God. It is the earth initiation, which is the culmination of your life in a physical body, and which was demonstrated to the world in the crucifixion of the Master.'

The Buddha describes this ultimate surrender as the moment of overcoming all suffering. It is often associated with light and dissolving into light and formlessness, but at the same time an ascension of form into perfection and perfect love. We see this in the accounts of the ascension of the Master Jesus.

We may not yet be at that stage of perfect love, but sometimes in meditation we can catch a glimpse of it through an awareness of selflessness and becoming one with all. It is often accompanied by light, and a love beyond anything we know on earth – yet it is something which inwardly we recognize.

Meditation for Non-Resistance

You see the lotus lying in the master's hands – its openness, its purity, serenity; its oneness.

See the lotus flower open in receptivity to all things, with the divine white fire at its heart, and see that light overflowing from the lotus cup in compassion for all. Surrender to the oneness of all life.

In the white lotus is the symbol of lack of separation and isolation. In resisting nothing you embrace all; in holding nothing to yourself you share all and become nothing; allness and nothingness are two sides of the same coin of creation.

All barriers are removed between you and the whole of creation, and you dissolve into the white light.

15. Resting

'PLEASE DON'T tell me to relax; it's only my tension that's holding me together!' said a student. So we won't tell you to relax, but instead to rest.

Relaxing is quite a physical thing, but it's more! It is not just a question of letting go, but of the deliberate letting go of something. What we let go of is the forceful striving of the consciousness. As we have already seen, the Taoists call this process *wuwei*, effortless effort.

Here is a relaxation exercise which encourages the release of the forceful mental consciousness. In its place one finds the heart's trust in the divine which upholds us. White Eagle says: 'Endeavour to get the feeling that the world is holding you up instead of you holding the world up. You will be surprised how much easier you feel. You cannot hold the world up, God does that. And God upholds you – whether you believe it or not, it is true. God is running your life, God is upholding you, if you let Him.'

Resting against the Invisible

When you are seated comfortably, or lying on a firm support, take your awareness to a place just below the back of your skull: to the top of your neck. Feel that you can soften there, and let that sensation travel down the neck, so that the neck muscles release and become slack. As you do this, feel also that the whole of the neck from the base of the skull broadens out to the sides, and that sensation goes all the way down the back: broadening, spreading, softening.

As this happens you may find yourself automatically taking a deeper breath. The chest will lift and open a little more, and the shoulderblades will drop. The whole back of the body is now released.

Then it feels as if the front of the body is resting against the back of your body – resting against something which you can't see, but you can feel as a strong support; the chest is spread, but not tight. The throat is calm and the muscles of the face spread out to the sides, the eyes deepen in their sockets, and the gaze becomes calm and relaxed.

The whole front of the body is resting back; the whole self has moved away from force, action, forward-seeking and striving, and it relaxes back into trust, into the support of the inner, invisible spine.

16. Stages of Meditation

BESIDES THE creation of form and the use of the senses, sometimes when we are learning to meditate, or even when we are experienced but finding it difficult (we all do that from time to time), it can help to break down the actual process of meditation into stages.

It could be said that there are three not wholly distinct, but independently describable stages which we go through in the process of any kind of inner spiritual contact, but particularly meditation.

1. The Releasing and Transitioning Stage

The first of the stages is the one in which we are releasing ourselves from the everyday world and entering a state which is receptive, open and relaxed. The transition from daily life, especially the everyday life of the mind, to a place of peace and stillness, is essential and often requires resolve. Sometimes, it is as if all the problems and decisions, major and minor, were just waiting for the moment when we sit still, to arise in our mind and trouble the waters of our emotions!

This is the point at which deeper or focused breathing, an inner focal point, or chanting the AUM, can be of most help. Focus, as we see, is the key here – in some manner we try to bring the mind under conscious control, but at the same time we are seeking to let go and relax as well, so the focus needs to be something which brings a feeling of relaxation: something which evokes beauty, a breathing practice which physically and etherically relaxes the heart, a sound which is harmonious and cuts through mental clutter. It can be seen that the focus is not on escape from the body, but on using the body to change the mental and emotional state.

The results of successfully changing our state at this stage are a feeling of relaxation (particularly the muscles of the neck, shoulders, solar plexus and face, which we can actually feel let go), a change in the breathing (this could be deeper, longer, or simply more aware) and a sense of stillness, calm, surrender, release, openness.

Although it is commonly hard to relax and let go of the earthly activity of the mind, sometimes this stage can occur very quickly. It's almost as if our higher self is totally ready and waiting for us just to leave the washing up, close the door and close our eyes – and then it immediately moves us through a state of relaxation towards the next stage.

In the Waiting Room

Waiting rooms are full of expectations. Imagine yourself sitting in a waiting room on the outskirts of the heaven world. Beyond an archway you can see a beautiful garden, and occasionally the scents waft into the room, with the sounds of laughter. You long to have the power to go through the arch, but you feel feeble. You imagine what you will find there – the greatest longings of your heart at this moment – the connection with God.

You look up at the sign on the wall in front of you, which says: 'The secret of strength lies in the quiet mind', and something clicks: if you wish to find the ability to transcend the heaviness of earth, you have to let go of all desire and all expectations of yourself and of what you will find.

You close your eyes to the room and the heavenly garden. You imagine yourself as a grail cup – the mind and feelings quite clear of all longing; just resting, completely contentedly, in this moment and just as you are. If there are thoughts in your mind about your ability, or anything which gets in the way of simply being, see those thoughts flowing out of your cup of awareness (see the next exercises) as you breathe out, until it is empty.

Simply be, and in that moment of acceptance you will be aware that God – all strength, wisdom and love – is within; that what appears to be empty is full of light!

2. The Focusing and Changing Thoughts Stage

Once we are in the receptive, peaceful state, with the mind more still, we can then lift our focus towards the spirit – towards the highest we can conceive, which is probably that ineffable light and spiritual being which creates all life. This is the stage at which our consciousness moves beyond the psychic to the spiritual. Indeed, this is the reason that in White Eagle's form of meditation we consciously focus on the Great Spirit.

Through merely having the thought of God, at this stage our consciousness inevitably spirals beyond the physical: upwards or inwards or outwards. This is where we lose the focus on the earthly body. We may no longer be aware of our breathing: rather, there may be a feeling of weightlessness, of being larger than life, or of expansion. At the same time, we may be aware of light and of a love beyond emotion. It is as if God reaches down towards us, as our mind reaches up, and that God enfolds us in comfort and belonging. This can produce a sense of profound trust. We may be reminded of the words, *Seek and ye shall find; knock and the door shall be opened to you*.

The focus on the Great Spirit is what allows our inner senses to open at the spiritual rather than the astral level. The inner senses may begin to stir with the beginning awareness of light, sound, colour, sense, and feeling – just in flashes or glimpses. However, this stage may be essentially formless, and it may well be just what is needed that we stay in this unstructured state of awareness for the rest of our time of meditation: simply, yet deeply, being with an awareness of God, in the light.

This is a stage of trust, and impatience or expectation at this point can get in the way. It may be good to know that meditation varies from time to time, according to our soul need – not always recognized by the mind – and sometimes being still in the light is the greatest need. If this is so, then this stage of meditation is the high point, and to be impatient about 'seeing' something or 'going' somewhere will only move our consciousness away from what can be a most profound stillness and quietude.

The Grail Cup

One of the great skills of meditation is being able to empty oneself of all preconceptions, all preoccupations and anything which will get in the way of the consciousness being raised. It is often a deliberate process of releasing. As you sit quietly at the beginning of your meditation time, you may be aware of tensions in the body and thoughts spinning in the mind. It is not very easy to empty the mind completely; in fact, White Eagle says it is not really possible, but we can learn to focus the mind on spiritual rather than earthly things.

A symbol that may be helpful is that of a chalice like the one used at the Last Supper. Picture this grail cup and imagine that you are that cup – indeed that every cell in your body is part of that holy receptacle. This is the point at which you have the intention to release as a deliberate act, so have the thought that with each outbreath the cup is emptying – all physical, unimportant things are draining out of you. You may indeed have the sensation of release and of opening out, the awareness of creating space within yourself.

Allow yourself to spread out into that space. Each outbreath is an opportunity to create and occupy that space within yourself, to let go of blockages and to reveal the golden chalice of the self, still radiant and open to receive. And now you can be aware of the light of God pouring down into the chalice of the self, filling every part with the eternal love of the spirit. As you become filled with this spiritual essence, so your consciousness changes and your spiritual senses awaken.

3. The Stage of Multi-Consciousness

However, should the inner senses continue to expand, we may find ourself moving into the next stage – a level of consciousness where past, present and future become irrelevant; where body, soul and spirit become as one. At this stage, with the opening of the inner senses, many different things can be experienced. The vision may open to reveal the garden of the spirit, where we can meet our loved ones who have passed over. Glimpses of a past life may come and go. We may be taken by our master or guide to a temple of healing, or a place where we receive understanding. Sounds and voices may be heard which are not of earth – the angelic realm may be revealed to us.

But there is something more which characterizes the essence of this stage: the senses seem to coalesce into one totality. There's an understanding which comes from all the spiritual senses, but is also more than the sum of them. We perceive divine truth with every part of our being. This may happen quickly, or it may be that we move to the heart of the temple, the heart of the lotus, the apex of the mountain, before we touch the edge of what is called cosmic consciousness. This moment can seem to last for a minute, and yet we may have sat for half an hour. Or in five minutes we can experience the whole of a past life, or float with the angels out among the stars for what seems like eternity.

It is worth reiterating that these stages are not completely distinct, and may not even be recognizable to some of us who are experienced – so fluid may be our transitions from one to the other – and it is important not to be caught up too rigidly in what we think 'should' be. Furthermore, a meditation is as it is. If we are open, and without any expectations or feelings of being 'not good enough', then any one of these stages may be the high point for us at a particular time. Whatever our need, it will be supplied, even if we are not totally aware of that need.

Finally, it can be seen that these stages are not restricted only to deliberate times of meditation. For example, being in the natural world can bring such relaxation that creative inspiration can arise. A beautiful scene can evoke an awareness of spirit so powerful that prayer springs to the lips and heart. And there are sublime moments when the conditions are just right internally and externally for the veil to be lifted suddenly, so that even while we are involved in earthly pursuits all the glory of the spiritual world is glimpsed. Perhaps this happens briefly, as if through a window, yet it is felt so deeply that in that moment we know we are spirit as well as matter.

'Meditation should be not something to be indulged in at odd moments spent in your sanctuary, but should fill your whole life, so that at all times there is consciousness of the Christ Light in the heart. It should be a continual awareness; and the purpose of life, the purpose of all striving, is that you may be aware of this divine love, this perfection of life, so that you live continually in harmony, in sweet happiness within – as Jesus did.'

17. The Mystery of Imagination

ULTIMATELY, at the heart of meditation there is a mystery. It is the mystery of our birth, our eternal life, of our relationship with God and with each other. It is the mystery of love.

To try to meditate without this understanding is to expect things to be known, seen, experienced with the outer self, rather than with that subtle inner knowing which is the intuition. That means we may expect a television presentation, even something like putting on 3-D glasses and seeing a holographic representation of a fantasy world. White Eagle is very clear about the use of the imagination:

'Many people have an intense appreciation of the beauties of nature, of the kingdom of nature where the infinite love of the Creator is revealed. Joy comes to the human heart through the beauty of the sky and the colours and the forms created by the clouds, the song of the birds and the perfume of flowers, the sound of nature, the perfume of nature, the glory of the rolling seas and the colour reflected in the water. Many people can recognize and enjoy all these beauties, but they cannot get beyond what the physical eyes are seeing. Yet there are some who are able to use their feeling, and as they stand lost in wonder before some scene of natural beauty, then through imagination they can feel the glorious presence of God beyond the physical form. When listening to music they can respond to sound reverberating through the universe, quite beyond the physical sound.

Through imagination, a person accustomed to express their soul in words is able to touch worlds remote from this one and to convey in words the vision vouchsafed to their higher mind and spirit.'

'It is important that we all recognize the value of imagination, because most people are so afraid of being deceived that they draw a heavy curtain between themselves and the real world of spirit. We tell you most earnestly that true imagination – please notice what we say – true and real imagination is the doorway into the etheric world, the doorway into the higher mental world and, beyond that, into the celestial or heavenly world, and even beyond again into the cosmic world.'

'In your meditations you are told to visualize. Remember what we have said. We will seek the altar in your temple. You are imagining a glowing, golden altar. This is real, this light which is being generated by you, rising in you. See it in the form of a blazing star. This is not imagination, but what you are creating by your aspiration, your will, by direction of your thoughts. You are building it yourself. You are causing this light to enter the chakras and they are opening like flowers.

'Sometimes you will hear a clairvoyant describe a lotus about the head of someone. If you are clairvoyant and see that, recognize it as a symbol of developing spiritual power. It means that the chakras are beginning to open instead of being shut tight and looking like dull discs. Through an effort of will, meditation and aspiration this is happening.

'Remember the tree of life that God planted in the Garden of Eden. As you proceed in spiritual unfoldment, your tree of life commences to open in bud and flower. God planted the tree in the East. Light comes from the

East. The pineal gland is the place of the East. If your eye (the pineal gland) is single and full of light, your whole body will be full of light.'

'These beautiful places are real. The astral atoms are formless until by the will of the aspirant they are brought into form. They are just as real on the astral plane as your not very beautiful places down here. When you hear people speaking lightly of imagination, remember they are making a big mistake. That which is created on the astral plane by imagination is real and true. These creations can be brought into being and can be dissolved, although form in the astral plane is more durable than down here, but you have to remember that in God's universe all is change. "Change and decay" – or shall we say the coming into form and the dissolving of form? What you have to realize in your meditation is that you are working with the substance of God, which is eternal. But form need not be eternal. In the altar of your being God has given you power to create form.'

'Those who would develop their spiritual gifts should never seek outside themselves for this development – for instance, by reading all kinds of occult literature advising this or that practice or procedure. It is far, far better to concentrate on meditation. Meditation will bring you the greatest help, first of all in controlling your emotions; and secondly it will help you to cultivate your imagination or the power of imagery – or, a better description, to create form on the etheric plane. With meditation goes training in right thought. So much harm is done by negative thought. Not only the emotions but also the thoughts must be controlled and directed into positive channels, positive thought, God-thought. This is why, in the work of the Brotherhood and the distant healing in the Lodge, you are not only serving your fellows but also developing your own spiritual gifts.'

Exercises in Visualizing

All of the exercises that follow are intended not only to give you practice in visualizing, but also are chosen specifically to enhance the awareness of all the inner senses. They are given in a sequential way, which introduces you to the various states of mind and feeling which meditation can bring, like peace, freedom, and so on. Each idea is based on White Eagle's teaching. It is advisable to be in as quiet a place as you can, where you won't be disturbed.

Take each one of the questions separately, closing your eyes after each one and picturing what you have read. Towards the end you might be surprised by how easy it is to go into a deep meditation. If this begins to happen, think of reaching for the highest spiritual plane, and afterwards follow the coming down and sealing ritual given on page 235.

• What is outside the place where you are? See it in your mind's eye.

• What is your favourite, or one of your favourite flowers? Where is it situated? What are its colours? Its perfume, if it has one?

• Which sound would you most like to hear right now, which would lift your heart? Where is that sound coming from, or from whom?

• Which natural perfume is most evocative or pleasing to you? Imagine where you would smell it.

- Which one of these makes you feel most still: a still flame, the still surface of a pool, the image of the meditating Buddha?
- Out of this list, what kind of place makes you feel most inspired and expansive: mountains, the sea, a starry sky at night, rolling hills covered in tall grass, a lake stretching into the distance, the sensation of floating out in space among the stars?
- Which of these makes you feel most free and which do you long to do: dance, fly, swim in an ocean, run?
- Which of the following makes you feel most refreshed and cleansed: a waterfall by a pool, a fountain, the gentle rain? Which do you most long to be under?
- If you could do one creative thing to your satisfaction – for example paint, sew, cook, write, sculpt, compose, sing, play an instrument, choreograph or dance – which would you choose?   .
- If you could go anywhere in the world, what place would you go to?
- Out of the list that follows, which kind of place would you choose to walk: among the pines, in an ancient woodland, in a grove of trees filled with beautiful blossom, in a young beechwood in the spring?   .
- Which of these would you find most beautiful to witness right now: the rising sun over the sea, the rising moon over the mountains, the unfolding petals of a flower in the sun in a warm garden, children playing in the world of spirit, the angelic life in a garden or wood?
- If you could visit one of these right now, which

would it be: a crystal temple with one special crystal at its centre, a temple of wisdom with mirrored walls and black and white squares on the floor, a small, simple, white sanctuary, a sacred grove, a stone circle in the mountains, an Egyptian temple of soft, warm sandstone and tall pillars, a cathedral, a monastery in the mountains?

•   If you could receive guidance and strength from one teacher or master right now, which one would it be?

18. Beauty as a Guide

WE HAVE SEEN from the previous exercise, based on some of the things he says, how White Eagle focuses on beauty. He tells us: 'Thought is creative; we work as far as possible on the creative power of thought. We try to avoid all destructive thought', he is giving us an indication of the direction in which our thoughts need to travel if we are to reach the highest levels of awareness in meditation.

'Many souls on earth declare it inadvisable to look for beauty and ignore what is ugly; and some may think that in these talks we draw too much attention to the beauty of the spiritual life and insufficiently enlarge upon the suffering and the ugliness of human life. We shall continue to present our subject in as beautiful a light as we can, believing that this best helps our brothers and sisters on earth, believing that the beam of light and beauty in the dark place of life is the surest, the finest and the best way of bringing the human mind into harmony with the divine Spirit. Of what use is it to stand in a dark room and contemplate the darkness? No progress is made thus; but if a lighted candle or lamp be brought into that room, it illumines and reveals all.'

In chapter 5, 'Remembering Who we really Are', we learnt about the importance of rising through the astral level to the highest. We have also seen how this process makes meditation different from visualization. Focusing on what is beautiful has the same effect as White Eagle's example given in another context in the last chapter: 'Send forth thoughts of devotion, which would find no response on the astral but would ascend to the celestial plane'. In other words, if we want to reach for the highest in our meditations, then beauty and devotion are two means to this end.

'With the coming of the Aquarian Age you will see a revolution in education, in religion, in science. Even now, there come influences which are stimulating certain advanced souls to bring into operation a new system of education. Instead of education being a process of intensive mental study, so that the mind becomes blocked and stuffy, the new influences will penetrate the spirit, the intuition of the children will be unfolded, and stimulated, but with] vibrations of beauty of colour, and art and form. The ear will be trained to hear beautiful music, the eye to see beauty. There will be beauty expressed throughout life.... Beauty: the external expression of the spirit; beauty, not the creation of intellect alone, but in itself an expression of the Divine.

'If you feel the beauty of the heaven worlds, you are receiving divine truth intuitionally. This is how you can discriminate between God's will and self-will. Having reached this understanding you can safely rely upon your intuition. It all comes to these few simple words: *Be still* (in love) *and know that I AM God*.

'The thing is for the spirit to remain unaffected by the challenge – that is the word we will use – the challenge of matter, of the lower life. Strive to respond to beauty and strive to feel love towards life. Let your heart be always in tune with the Infinite Love. If you can live in this manner, you will be living your meditation.

'We beg you to gain a more comprehensive view of the process of spiritual growth in men and women, remembering always that God's plan is to bring beauty. I will not say perfection, not in the limited sense in which the word is understood. To us there is no standing still; even with God, we do not see a perfected Being, completely finished and there for ever…. We wonder at and worship a God ever growing more beautiful, ever sending forth greater waves of life and light, expressing Himself, Herself, not only in this universe, but in universes yet unborn. As this growth of the divine spirit takes place, so also is there development in each one of the individual life spirits of which you are one, the growth of creative powers within you, and increasing harmony and attunement of each individual spirit to the Father–Mother God.'

What this focus on beauty also does is to transform. We all have experience of physical things which seem inherently ugly being transformed when light shines on them. Or perhaps there is a connection between the object and someone we love, and the association changes our perspective. The same is true in meditation: we are helped to realize (make real for ourselves) the beauty which is intrinsic to the heaven world and the higher states of consciousness, and because all states are one, that realization permeates right down to the incarnating part of the self. We experience and become more beautiful on every level.

Realizing and Creating Beauty: Meditative Exercise

Sit quietly and think of the things in life which you find beautiful. Imagine the most beautiful colours, scenery, music, form. Notice how these things are not necessarily known as beautiful by the world, but are the things you love.

If you had to choose a flower or a tree to represent beauty, what would you choose? With your eyes closed, picture this flower or tree as clearly as you can, but in bud against a grey sky, or as a shoot or sapling pushing up from the dark earth.

There may be a part of your life which feels ugly; or even a part of yourself. Acknowledge this, but then place that symbol of beauty – the bud of the flower; the sapling – in the place in yourself or your life that feels ugly. Imagine yourself receiving that symbol into your open hands, or placing that symbol in your life, as you would place a plant in the soil.

Gradually, as you breathe gently, see that beauty coming to maturity. See the bud unfolding in perfection; see the tree growing strong and lovely in the sunlight.

Now take your mind back to the ugliness you perceived in yourself or your life and see it transformed. In whatever way is appropriate, see the change from ugliness to beauty: not necessarily a change in form but certainly a change within your perception.

Hold onto that thought during your daily life and whenever you feel the sadness or criticism of ugliness creeping in, picture the flower or the tree in full radiance, and know that this is the spiritual truth behind all the illusion of earthliness and karma.

The Beauty of the Inner Garden

White Eagle says:

'In this method of meditation, after we have made that initial contact in the golden light at the apex of the mountain, you are instructed to use the creative imagination in order to visualize in the soul world a most perfect and beautiful garden – the infinite and eternal garden.

'In creating a garden in the inner worlds we have a wide choice of season and setting. For instance, it may be springtime in your garden, or high summer with all its rich colour and life; we might see the garden set in a perfect landscape with majestic trees, flowering shrubs and herbaceous borders; or with rock gardens and a running brook of pure clear water through which can be seen stones like jewels, and fish of different colours; there may be smooth green lawns, or a blue lake.

'In these surroundings we are able to use our creative imagination to develop our spiritual senses. As we observe the light and life in all the beautiful form before us, we develop our spiritual sense of sight; and we develop our spiritual sense of sound as we listen to the song of birds, the trickle of water in the brooks and waterfalls, the music of the gentle wind in the trees. We can develop our spiritual sense of smell as we inhale the pungent freshness of the earth and the subtle perfumes of the variety of flowers, some of which may be unknown to us on earth. We develop, too, our spiritual sense of taste as in imagination we try the fruit from bush, tree and vine, and cup our hands to sip the fresh sweet water; our sense of touch as our hands are immersed in that cool water, or laid upon the living stones which edge the lily pool.'

'Sometimes you can make contact with your loved ones who have passed into the next state of life. Those dear friends of yours are now living in a world of sunlight, an intensely beautified earthly state. If you could draw aside the heavy curtain of materiality, you would look into a world of perfection, into a sunlit life of harmony, softness – where there can be activity, and also passivity, when the soul desires it, or seeks to rest. Then there are spheres beyond the astral, spheres of great activity, where beings who have passed through all the grades of the lower life have now found freedom of action, so that they can follow the particular ray of their soul, where they can study the heavens if they so desire, or can study music or art, literature or sculpture. Any great longing of the soul is there given expression. Such spheres are infinitely more beautiful than anything you can conceive while you are imprisoned in your box of flesh. Remember, although imprisoned, your box is similar to a radio box. You have knobs you can turn, and can tune in to other realms.'

Creating your own
Infinite and Eternal Garden

Having read White Eagle's words, use any aspect which appeals to you to create your perfect garden, or natural scene in your mind. You will find the mind wanders, so choose one object or sensation which you can return to each time the mind has wandered off. (Of course, you might find you wander off into that garden, which will be delightful!)

The Mother Energy

'In this garden we may feel the presence of the divine Mother – truly the spirit of motherhood. And it is the realization of this all-enfolding love, compassion and tenderness that makes the deepest and most lasting impression upon us as we meditate in the infinite and eternal garden.'

'In the western world, reference to the divine Mother is assumed to be to Mary, mother of Jesus. But the ancients would say that the Mother, the great Mother Earth, was another aspect of God the Father, the two in one, the parents of humanity, and thus the picture of a dual deity emerges. If one thinks of the Father as the spiritual as well as the physical sun and the Mother as giving form to all life – the corn, the fruit, the trees, the flowers, the creatures – then one can see why the ancients worshipped God, the Father, as the Creator, the energy, and God the Mother, the womb in which the seed of life is nurtured by the warmth of the sun.'

'To those who know her, the appearance of divine Mother in meditation is not infrequent. She comes as the spirit of the beautiful and perfect woman. She is woman made perfect, even as Christ is man made perfect. As you conceive the attributes and the qualities of the Christ in a man, so does the divine Mother manifest as a personality in the perfect form, beauty and attributes of a mother.

'To each nationality she normally appears as one of their own race. Therefore, to a European she will appear as such, very beautiful in face and form, clothed in the softest white flowing robes, with a cloak of heavenly madonna blue. An aura of light comprising all the softest colours of the spectrum radiates from her, and the sweet subtle perfume of roses. She is beautiful beyond compare. She is universal spirit taking the human form of a mother because it is the easiest way to come very close to all her children on earth, to help them, to comfort them in time of sorrow, bitterness or loneliness. Through her human–divine personality she reaches right down into the very depths of the human heart. We all yearn for a mother's love, a mother's understanding, and in the divine Mother we find the comfort and deep spiritual peace which is the culmination of life and happiness.'

'In the invisible universe are the most wonderful, beautiful things. We cannot tell you, or describe them, simply because you haven't yet the capacity to even imagine these things. Imagination, or the power of imagery, is really the power of the creator working in you. You visualize, or you create an image. That image can only be representative of the degree of development of the God within you. Then of course you must remember that there are so many aspects of beauty. Only a very infinitesimal part of the glory of God's creation is visible until you have unfolded and developed the spiritual powers to see, which means to create.'

19. Mindfulness and More

MEDITATION in the White Eagle Lodge is not just about being mindful, but about touching the divine mind and allowing it to unfold within the earthly consciousness. The mind of heaven reveals and unfolds itself within the mind of earth through stillness and focus. Meditation is also about creativity of the highest kind.

Changing the Brain

What helps provide the impetus to meditate? Well, to start with we are bigger and wiser than our brains. In order to meditate, we need to encourage the brain to understand the importance of what we are doing, so that it switches from its default mode of seeking to initiate action, into a focused, introspective mode.

It is necessary to think of this beforehand, so that we don't enter meditation unprepared, like a teenager reluctantly forced to revise, for example, but rather as we would focus on a task we love – a game, an episode in a story, doing something creative yet relaxing, which requires our awareness and requires us to be in the moment.

The brain is designed to do everything it can firstly to keep us safe and then to make life work for us in the best way possible. So it needs to know that our health, well-being and efficacy in daily life are all going to be increased through meditation. This means that we have to believe in the importance of meditation to us, personally and wholeheartedly – in other words, so that we see meditation as a carrot, not a stick. The stick will bring resistance and strain.

As we saw earlier, one thing which helps is to be aware of the positive changes in us when we meditate, especially when we come out of the meditation, so that we help the brain to understand the benefits and become aware of how we really do change in consciousness for the better, and in efficacy.

It also helps to practise being present in each moment – in other words, not to be somewhere else in our mind and feelings, but engaged with this moment at every level. From that engagement one can move forwards. It's a bit like engaging the gears in a car: without engaging them, we are in uncontrolled motion and cannot progress where we want to go. To be present in each moment means to bring one's attention to the things of the moment, which is why so many meditation practices revolve around focusing on an object, a mantra, the breathing, or the body itself in some way. The more we practise at different times in the day, the easier this becomes when we decide to meditate.

Creating Mental Space

Imagine yourself standing or sitting in a light but empty room with French windows open to the garden beyond. It is summer and the scents of flowers and grass flow into the room.

There is space all around, and a sense of freedom,

with the garden full of soaring birds and a backdrop of hills against the wide, open sky.

There is no clutter, no expectations on your time; there are no things to worry about.

As you breathe in the sweet air coming from the garden, allow space between each breath, and as you do this allow that there is a corresponding space between your thoughts.

Continue for as long as you like, and then take the attention away from the breath.

The Mind in the Heart: the Entrance to Heaven

In mentioning the White Eagle Heart Meditation, on p. 21, we shared from a White Eagle teaching some words about the centrality of the heart chakra. In the same teaching, White Eagle goes on to show how we cannot be too rigid in our thinking about spiritual matters. He assures us that through the heart we are actually linked with the higher mind. This means that we are able to reach a higher state of consciousness than is possible through focus on the lower mental levels.

At the same time, this supports the knowledge that the higher planes are those we are aiming for, and demonstrates again the difference between visualization, and the power of true, spiritual imagination: 'In order to help you understand the unity of life we try to help you to turn inward, to find the entrance to heaven through your own spirit, your own heart; for you will only find entrance to the heaven world through your heart chakra – or rather, through the point of union between the heart and the higher mind, between the heart chakra and the head chakras. When this union between heart and head has come about you will have learnt the secret of reaching the heaven world. The heaven world is neither "here" nor "there": it is everywhere; it is within yourself.'

What is the 'higher mind'? It is the will to will the Will of God; it is the aspiration to love. The heart is the seat of the spirit. The head centre is the seat of the soul. Christ-consciousness, or heaven, is when soul and spirit become one, just as they do to a degree when we die.

In a chapter in his book, THE SNOW LEOPARD, Peter Matthiessen describes Sakyamuni's path to enlightenment and the finding of his Buddha nature. Matthiessen mentions 'a place of transcendent knowing which is only found in the transparent radiance of the stilled mind'. It is 'that higher consciousness which is in all sentient beings' (what White Eagle would call 'the mind in the heart'). The passages in this chapter which follow all refer to the importance of the heart.

In referring to far memories, for example, White Eagle says: 'These memories do not come through the earthly brain, so much as through the spiritual brain, centred in the heart. It is through the mind in the heart that contact with eternity is made. It is another name for intuition.'

'When does the mind in the heart commence to function, then? Only when the soul of a man or woman commences to be. That is, the soul to be, instead of the mind to think. Yet the mental man or woman knows everything, can explain theology, grasp all the religions of the past and present! And yet they are empty; these things mean nothing unless the mind of the heart is functioning. The learning gleaned from books and facts must be enriched by human kindliness.

'To become part of the great universe of God, that heart centre has to grow, to radiate affection, to burn as a great fire in the individual soul. The soul has to live, not for itself and its own glorification, but to serve and minister to other beings, healing the sick and comforting the sorrowful, feeding the hungry. A person's religion must express itself in practical service on earth. Then the heart mind is functioning.'

'The individual, the microcosm, is a universe and the centre or the sun of that universe is the heart, not the head. As the sun is the central point for your solar system, so your heart is the centre of your universe. The spiritual counterpart of the physical sun is the Christ Light; when that also is awakened in the heart, the heart mind commences to function. The physical sun rules the physical heavens, and the Christ rules through the sun, or the heart of each human being, the destiny of humanity and of the earth.'

Meditation on 'the Point of Union between the Heart and the Higher Mind'

Imagine the heart centre being aflame with love, maybe by visualizing a flame within a lotus or a rose…. The tip of the flame is reaching up to the brow; to the mind….

Have the feeling that the ordinary mind, the mind of every day, is opening, letting go, becoming still so that the warmth of the flame can awaken the higher mind – the inner will and wisdom….

The heart's light and the mind's light merge …

And now reach up through the crown….

The flame from the heart warms and brightens the mind, dissolving narrow, dark thoughts and expanding the consciousness….

The vision opens to perceive and become aware of heavenly things…

The Meditation Mind

'We want you to understand that you can create infinite beauty because the divine mind in you can manipulate the white ether. People who do not understand will think this is all imagination and that nothing created in this way is real. But the ether is a very real substance, more real than physical matter, and the higher or divine mind in you can mould that sensitive ether into living form.'

'When you meditate, if you are working correctly, you will be conscious only of more beautiful and harmonious conditions of life. These you will be able to see, to hear, to feel, to taste and to smell with your etheric senses. When meditating, you are not only thinking or contemplating abstractly; with your higher mind you are creating a condition of life in which at that moment you are living and participating. Do understand this. You are being led step by step along the path into those higher worlds of harmony and peace, truth and wisdom. But it is not an abstract condition; it is a world of form in which you are living during your meditation.

'In a led meditation, your leader may give you a picture to imagine or think about; perhaps lovely mountain peaks, and one in particular which is capped with the golden light.

By certain ritual your leader helps you to rise until you are in a higher state of consciousness on the mountain peaks. In another meditation, you may be taken to the infinite and eternal garden. Through the ritual used you are bringing into operation a mind above the normal consciousness, superior to all normal, ordinary thought.

'This is the mind which is used in meditation, and the description given to you of that heaven world, which your higher mind or superior mind takes up, and which becomes for you a real world during your meditation. If what you are seeing and experiencing is beautiful and inspiring, and makes you feel at peace with your fellow beings and all life, then surely that must be good, and an aspect of life to be encouraged and developed. You need not fear intrusion or darkness, for if the thought and aspirations are pure, you are always protected by the power of God, which is all good, all love.'

The Diamond Self

Although, as White Eagle tells us, the heart is the central point of the chakra system, in meditation all the chakras are stimulated. This obviously includes the throat and the brow centres. The diamond self refers to the brow centre – not that from which the lower mental operates, but the higher mind – the mind which, when stimulated to any degree, brings vision, intuition, and leads to clairvoyance of the highest quality. White Eagle calls this faculty 'inspiration', which is interesting in itself because of the emphasis he also places on what he calls God-breathing. To be inspired is to breathe in harmony with the Sun.

The diamond reflects and refracts the light. It needs

to be pure to do this, otherwise there is distortion of the impressions we are receiving. As has been said, one reason for taking our thoughts to the highest, or God, first, is to reach the pure planes of consciousness through focus on the divine. In that way our meditation is less likely to be simply astral visualization, or open to the possibility of misrepresentation.

Lifting the Thoughts
into Clarity and Beauty

To begin this meditation, focus on breathing in the light, perhaps with the thought, 'I breathe in light, I breathe out peace'. Feel the heart centre of divine love expanding in light with each breath.

And as in the last exercise, visualize the light in the form of a flame, the radiance from which gradually reaches up to the brow. As you focus on the brow, bringing your inner attention to that chakra, which is just above and between the eyes, imagine a clear diamond resting there, and the light from the flame penetrating and reflecting from the beautiful, clear crystal surfaces.

Feel your mind becoming and more and more still, until 'the transparent radiance of the stilled mind' – that lovely phrase of Peter Matthiessen's – takes over your consciousness, and you are raised into the higher mental world of true vision.

20. The Power of What we Think

IN ORDER to understand how and why the imagination is so powerful, we need to become aware of what White Eagle says about the immense importance of thought and its power to transform. In the passages that follow, White Eagle explores the reality of thought not only as a prelude to action, but as an influence on physical life in itself. It is interesting that medical scientists and sports psychologists are realizing more and more that just imagining or thinking something can, with time, have an effect – for example, on the ability to perform better, without having moved a muscle!

'An important lesson which all have to learn is the power of thought. You are living an outer life in a physical world. But side by side with this outer life there is an inner life. This inner life is a world of thought and thought provokes action. Now, 'as a man thinks, so he becomes' – he or she is creating an inner world of their own. From that inner world come their speech and action. When you withdraw from your physical body at night and rise, perhaps only a little distance, from your physical body, you enter a world of thought. When the spirit finally leaves the body, it goes into what is described as an inner world that has been created by thought. Thought is the impetus; it is the seed of action. So, obviously, if you look for a heaven world that is beautiful and peaceful, you must strive to attain that world of beauty and peace within yourself, within your soul, in your thoughts, because this is the world that awaits you when you die.

'At this very moment, you have opportunities to purify your thoughts, to live in a world of beauty. Remember that thought creates form. Imagination is a creative power; and if the inner world, your soul world, is beautiful, if you have beautiful thoughts of God and God's creation, the creative power which is yours will take and mould the finer ether of the next world into beautiful form.'

'Once we fully grasp the power of thought, we can use this to shape our lives in beauty and harmony. What you send forth must be repaid, and so you serve a double purpose when you train yourself to think kindly and constructively. This, like the law of karma, is absolute and scientific.'

'We would make this clear: every thought goes forth from your mental body with a wave-like action and finds a corresponding vibration in the ether. Science is only on the outermost fringe of comprehension of the power of thought. Thought can do anything in this world. It forms the root of all suffering and of wars. Thought can also be the foundation of beauty and harmony and brotherhood and bring all that you long for. Thought is creative; we work as far as possible on the creative power of thought.

We try to avoid all destructive thought. We make it a rule in giving advice and help always to construct, to see nothing but good; we may be called foolish optimists; but we know that by seeing only good, creating good in our positive thought we will help to bring about the thing which is desirable and good. We do not see or think in terms of pessimism, destruction or death. All is life, all is unfolding, all is ever progressing. All is good, all is God.'

Creating your Affirmation

A POSITIVE affirmation is a way to change your thoughts and your feelings for the better. As you affirm, part of you may think, 'But I'm not…!'. This doesn't really matter: what an affirmation does is to affirm your true self and be a magnet for the highest within you.

Choose a time of day when you will focus on the affirmation you create. It needs to be relevant to you, present-centred and positive, and when you repeat it, it needs to be said in a way which focuses on the words and their meaning, rather than just repetition of sound. Below are some examples.

You are telling yourself, 'There is a state of mind beyond what I am thinking right now, where all is resolved.' Imagine your mind reaching out towards that shining peak or place of freedom with the phrase you choose:

- *I am not this limited body that I inhabit*
- *I am not this mind*
- *I am not these feelings*
- *I breathe in peace; I breathe out love*
- *I am safe; all is well*
- *I let go, and open my heart and mind to receive healing*
- *I am spirit, and spirit is eternal*
- *Within me is the Christ light which can overcome all … [fear, pain, sorrow, guilt, illusion, confusion, etc.]*
- *I am surrounded by loving help*
- *Death is an awakening to a more beautiful life*
- *I can lose nothing and no one; I will always be in touch with those I love*

- *This moment is perfect, and from it I can grow in …* *[peace, love, strength, well-being, joy, etc.]*
- *In my darkest moments I am closest to God*
- *My spirit is strong and knows my need; all is as it should be*
- *I can trust myself*
- *My body is only part of me; I live beyond it*
- *I surrender to the rightness of this moment*
- *The power of God upholds me; there is nothing to fear*
- *I am more than this pain*
- *My loving, listening presence is powerful, and just what is needed*
- *I release my feelings of … [fear, anger, hurt, resentment, bitterness, despair, etc.]; I breathe in love*
- *God's love is unconditional; I am safe*
- *I free my loved one, knowing we will never be parted*
- *I go forwards into the light with joy*

Habitual Thoughts

'What you think habitually, your way of thought or tendency to either good thought or destructive thought, is far, far more important than you allow. This is another reason why meditation is the path along which the aspiring soul is guided, because in meditation is created a power of stillness and receptivity to spiritual forces. As the spiritual forces flow into the soul and the body, they help to train the power of thought in normal life.'

'Development of the mental body depends upon your habitual thought. We mean by this the building or development of the higher mental vehicle through which the

Christ within can and will operate, so as to create a world so far removed from and above this earth that it will not be of the same substance. Think of yourselves as descending like a babe to this earth in order not only to develop in yourselves the qualities of the Son of God, but in the process to help all people to develop and to look towards the Great Light for their happiness and their redemption.'

'It is one thing to know with your mind and it is another thing to know with your inner self. To know in this fashion with your inner self means spontaneous good thought and spontaneous good action. It means a spontaneous giving forth of that light which is Love, which is creative, which is raising the very atoms, the very vibrations of your world.'

Through the process of meditation upon higher things, upon beauty, love and harmony, we are not only aiding our own development but, as White Eagle says, we are raising the vibrations of the whole world.

The World of Thought and Feeling

'Let us consider this inner world of which we speak. To you it will appear a mental world because when you withdraw from the outer, the physical life, you seem to go inward. Then it appears that you are living in your mind. Indeed you are often told that when you pass over you will be living in a mind world, but this is not only a world of thought but also a world of feeling. Thought is the next level to the physical. You are getting beneath thought. Thus you come to a world of finer feeling, or an emotional world.

'Although they do not recognize it, all people live in such a world, a world of emotion, and this emotional life is also affected by the mental world around them, or by the thoughts of others. Therefore, it becomes part of your training or development of spiritual insight, of clairvoyance and spiritual illumination, for you to learn to protect your fine emotional body from the harsh thoughts of the outer world. For you are unconsciously influenced by the thoughts of others.

'We are not suggesting, of course, that every upset of this nature is due to this emotional impact, but it sometimes happens…. It is one of the very first lessons to be learned – the recognition of the reality of this emotional plane, of your own emotional, your feeling body. You think with your mind, but you feel with this emotional body…. In the degree that you can call forth that mild, peaceful, tranquil love in your heart towards life – not only to people but towards life itself, so that you are radiating love – you are encircling your aura with a white shield which is impenetrable by the world. Unwanted thoughts cannot penetrate your aura if you have sent forth love from the temple, the centre in your heart. If your emotions are controlled, calm and lovely, you cannot be affected, nor your mind be disturbed by thoughts from the world.'

Here White Eagle describes a circle: positive thought leading to radiating love, which in turn brings the mind to a place where it is less disturbed by the world. What follows is how he then links this with what we do in meditation – which enables self-possession to happen, particularly through the light to be found in the well of stillness deep in the heart.

'In meditation, although you sit quietly, you may not immediately make contact with spirit. Spirit and mind are not wholly attuned, so you pick up all the thoughts and thought forms floating about in the ether. Meditation is not a nebulous, dreamy affair, but active. What you have to do is to bring what we call the higher will into operation. Beneath all thought is a place of consciousness receptive to divine power, which is the spiritual point of contact. This is not in the brain, but deep in the heart. In meditation it is as if you are looking deep, deep, deep into a well. Shining in the darkness is a tiny point of light. That is an awareness deep in your soul. Thoughts will still keep popping into your mind – but every time this happens withdraw again into your deep well of silence, of stillness. You will gradually become so conscious of it that you will grow strong, and it will become easier to find awareness of spiritual life. Go slowly, step by step, and remember, through your contact with that point of light, of spiritual consciousness, you will learn in time to control thought power.'

The Violet Ray: Meditative Exercise

Lie on your back somewhere comfortable, and close your eyes. When you are ready, take your attention to the rhythm of your breathing, the sensation of the breath coming and going in your body: the rise and fall of your chest; the feeling of expanding outwards as you breathe in and surrendering as you breathe out.

Feel this rhythm like the undulating movement of the waves. Imagine you are lying on top of the waves, quite safely … feeling their rise and fall beneath you.

The water is a deep, rich blue. The sensation is one of gentle, rhythmic, soothing peace, like a baby being rocked in its cradle.

You feel so safe in this spiritual ocean, which is like the earthly sea but not at all dangerous, that when you begin to sink gently into it, you let yourself go with trust. In this realm you know you will be able to breathe, no matter what.

As you sink down beneath the waves, the breath continues its easy flow in your body, but now the movement and sound of the waves recedes above you. You look up and can see the surface of the water – the turbulence and the energy of it – but you are moving deeper down into an ocean which is gradually changing colour all around you, becoming an ethereal and uplifting violet hue; the exact shade that appeals to your soul. The ocean doesn't feel like water at all but has become an enfolding warmth – a sensation of lightness and freedom and joy.

You rest in this violet light, being aware of the fears and anxieties which usually cloud your aura now floating above on the surface of your consciousness, while you absorb the healing courage and trust of the violet ray. As you are aware of the fears, so they evaporate from the surface in the strength of the sun.

When you wish, become aware of your breathing, and feel the rhythm of the breath carry you upwards towards the surface of your daily life again. Take your time, and keep the sense of being held by the Great Spirit in complete safety. When you are ready, become aware of where you are lying in your home; of your earthly body strong and resilient; and of your mind clear and at peace. Before you open your eyes, see yourself lying at the centre of a cross of light encircled by protective light.

I AM SAFE. ALL IS WELL.

21. Walking our Meditation
– as Above, so Below

SO FAR IN our exploration of White Eagle's teaching
on meditation, we have shown that the physical and the
spiritual are not separate but interpenetrating. We have
discussed the way in which poise and uprightness, along
with developing our sensory abilities, can help us to unfold spiritual awareness through the principle, 'As above,
so below'. By the same token, although for the most part
White Eagle meditation takes place sitting (or, if necessary,
lying down) there are many ways in which we can 'cultivate meditation' while walking, particularly in nature, even
under the night sky. He says:

'You will understand from this talk how important it is
to cultivate meditation. This does not mean to sit for hours
and hours and meditate upon oneself but rather to meditate as you go about the world, not letting this head brain
be always uppermost. Sometimes, in the country, when
walking through the lanes, endeavour to become in tune
with the eternal life behind the manifestation of trees and
flowers; meditate upon the grandeur and glory of God's
Universe so that the heart becomes active.'

'Some will take a country walk, and see very little. They
stay unaware of the beauties of nature. They have not reflected their surroundings. Another soul will take that same
walk and will become aware of maybe a thousand little
details apparent to it in the hedgerow and fields, in the bird

life, in the sunlight, in the shadow, and in the atmosphere. They will note many details, and are not merely observant with the physical eye, but with the spiritual eye also.

'Conceive a third man taking that same walk. He has become more sensitive still to the spiritual life behind the physical form, and his sight has greatly increased. He will not only see all the details of a physical nature, but also become aware of the pulsation or vibration of life and great beauty which permeates the physical manifestation. His soul will reflect the spirit world.'

'Look up, my friends, to the harmonies of the universe, and you will see beauty enfolding you. But you will not find such beauty through mental gymnastics or analysis; but only if you listen to the sounds (not noises): the harmonies in the universal life. To get near to heaven, leave the lowlands and climb a hill, or better still, a mountain. Be alone, listening; observe the life of nature, and from outward recognition and realization of the universal life, look inwards. Try to realize the relationship between the outer mysteries and the life of the within.'

Seeing the Spiritual Life Force in Nature

If you can, take a gentle walk somewhere you love, and when ready choose a part of the scenery around you as your focal point. Whatever natural phenomenon is the subject of your focus, let it be something beautiful to you, and have the intention in your mind that you will be 'seeing' the light, or life force, within nature.

In the world of spirit, in the gardens there, one is

aware of every blade of grass, leaf and stem shining with an inner light, which seems to extend outwards, but doesn't mask the beauty of the colour, rather enhances it. It is something like the light through stained glass windows.

As you contemplate your natural world, have in your mind's eye this idea. Imagine what the light in nature would look like. Imagine the light radiating out beyond the plant a little, like an aura. Focus on one aspect of nature, and try to relax the mind, so that you enter a dreamy state where all is possible – and of course it is not only possible, but is there.

When you can do this, if only for a fraction of time, you will be entering a state in which you can also become aware of the agents of that life force, the elementals and the angels of form. Have faith that they are there, and gradually in that light you may glimpse movement, or you may instead feel sudden joy which is one of the feelings which the nature spirits bring.

Becoming One with All Life

On another walk, choose a tree as the focal point. It would be possible, of course, to lie on the grass, or sit next to a rock instead, but a tree brings the feeling of both solidity and fluidity.

Stand or sit with your back to the tree and become aware, as in the previous exercise, of the life force in every part, and particularly how it rises up the trunk from the roots. Imagine this force flowing up and out to every branch, twig and leaf.

At the same time, feel that the life-force also rises in you, from beneath your feet, up the spine, and into every cell of your body.

As you think of the tree and yourself, again imagine or visualize the life force extending out beyond the tree and yourself, until those forces blend and become one.

Hold the image and thought of being one with the tree – not that you become it, but rather your two energies are part of a greater energy, the vibration of life itself.

If you can feel this, if only briefly, you may also then be in the vibration which the angels are aware of – the cosmic consciousness which is the realm which they inhabit.

It is then that you may sense the angel and elementals specifically connected with the tree.

If we repeat these exercises often, whenever we are taking a walk, gradually we will find that the inner world becomes more believable as a reality. In turn it will make it easier for us to touch those higher vibrations when we meditate, and to get glimpses into what White Eagle calls 'the heaven world'.

22. A Guiding Relationship

IN MEDITATION we may also feel the presence of those who are without physical bodies, yet who are close to us. They might be those who have been dear to us in this life, or those who are sometimes known as our guides. In that other place of our true home we meet with them sometimes in our sleep state, and whether we see them or not, we can often feel them with us in meditation.

As we learn to find heaven while still on earth, it is helpful to realize just how much of our soul is in existence in the spirit world. As White Eagle says in chapter 5, 'Remembering Who we Really Are': 'It is very difficult for you to recognize that you are not the little you that you think you are – that you are part of a more beautiful soul than you can conceive. That soul is your true self. Thus only a small part of you is here functioning through your body, while your inner self is attached at all times to that greater self.'

Since so much of who we really are is in spirit, when we seek to contact that greater soul, or experience the inner worlds, even when we just have the intention to be still and let God be present, we will be helped by both the angels and our spirit guides. White Eagle says:

'It is vitally important for every soul to make its own effort and aspire. According to the degree of that effort, you are helped onward and upward by your guide and teacher. It is not good complacently to leave all the work to your guide, which is a mistake many people make. It is

your duty to do the best you can. According to your physical equipment you ought to perfect the gifts which God
has given you, using your own effort; but remembering
that however perfect you make your brain and however much knowledge you acquire, you are only an instrument; for until you learn the magical secret of connecting
yourself with the spiritual current, you will remain empty.
As soon as you can make your connection, you open the
window of your soul. As you do this, or in other words
as you spiritually unfold your powers, you are able to see
and to feel the presence of those guiding you from the
higher planes. Every one of you here has your own guide
and angel helpers.'

White Eagle is keen to help us get away from the need
to categorize and name things, indicating that this is lim-
iting, and that spiritual truth cannot be contained completely or correctly in earthly terms. 'You understand that
when we are endeavouring to put these heavenly truths
into words we are at a loss. We can only hint. We can only
say things that will stir and quicken your minds and hearts
so that you will catch a train of thought or intuition and
follow that intuition.

'Spiritual truth is fluid. You can get principles upon
which to work, but truth is like a great river with many
tributaries. You will get sidetracked, you may get lost, but
always you come back to the main theme, the main principle. If you can rise above the earth and look down, you will
see where all the tributaries flow, see them all fit into the
grand panorama of beautiful life on earth, the Garden of
Eden.... When you do not understand spiritual truth, my
dear ones, do not worry; leave it. If you do not understand,
know that it is because you lack the capacity at present, but

you will have it. All will be revealed in due course. When you want to docket everything and tie truth up in neat little parcels, you will stumble.'

This applies to naming our guide, but more than this, even to recognizing them in one particular form. Most of the time, if we are aware of our guide in meditation he or she will appear in one 'dress', possibly one kind of form which is familiar to our soul. However, there can be occasions when they will appear differently and for a specific purpose – a different look and even a different gender.

'When we speak of guides, very often we mean helpers. You have many helpers during life who come from time to time to assist you through some particular period. You have only one particular teacher and guide, who may be attached to you through a number of lives. This spiritual teacher contacts you at a much higher level than the helpers. You receive his or her guidance through your conscience, or the voice of your higher self, sometimes called the voice of God. That still, small voice within can become very strong. It can become for you the voice of your spiritual teacher contacting you on the highest level of your earthly consciousness – or the highest level that you can attain whilst imprisoned in the flesh. All that is lovely and pure and true will come through from your higher self, and that is the level on which your spiritual teacher works.'

White Eagle adds: 'You think of your guide as being someone who lived a long time ago, and who comes to help you. That is true to a certain extent; but you, the real you, are linked to your guide or your teacher in a very certain way; indeed, we would almost say that you are inseparable and yet you are separate. It is difficult. Your guide is your highest self; and that highest self has other personalities. Your guide is really your teacher – because your teacher is your highest self, but not yourself. Your guide is so intimately related to your highest self as to be part of your highest self.

'The more advanced an ego becomes, the more it becomes at one with the whole, and does not know separation. Your guide is so much *en rapport* with your higher self that it is actually part of yourself, and knows no separation, except when you manifest as a much lower being than you actually are. When on the higher plane of true self, you are at one with your teacher. You breathe as one, you are one.'

'You recognize them from the feeling they bring, and again that inner knowing. Sometimes you will have what is called a guide described and you will say, "I am very happy to know my guide". At another time someone else describes another guide, so you have two guides. Later on you may have also a third guide described. By this time you are a little confused. All these descriptions may be of the one spirit, who, according to the vibrations and conditions prevailing at the time, will clothe himself or herself in garments of a past incarnation. The guide can put on the dress of the body of an Indian or an Egyptian or an Atlantean according to the conditions prevailing.'

The purpose of our guide or helper is not to tell us what to do. How can they, when the decisions we make are all about our learning; the outworking of our own karma? So one might ask what their role is in our earthly life. Our guide is a reminder. When we realize their presence, we are instantly reminded of our soul, which is much greater than the earthly being. As White Eagle says, our soul does not incarnate in entirety, and our guide is connected with our soul and has been over many lifetimes.

'Does it matter very much whether you can prove that the voice that is speaking is a separate entity, if that voice is giving you something which is helpful and elevating, if it is helping you to rise above the darkness of earth? Even if it is your own higher self, does it matter? That is the real point. We feel there is a little too much docketing and putting into pigeonholes with these things. Whatsoever is good and true and beautiful, accept and ponder in your heart.'

Thus it is as if that contact with the guide opens the door for our higher self to manifest more closely at the earthly level, and this means that whatever earthly struggle, decision or need there is, the higher self will be able to show the way forwards. This could be, and quite often is, simply a change of feeling inwardly; where there has been doubt, a sense of rightness; where there has been anxiety, a sense of peace; where there has been hopelessness, a sense of determination – and so on.

This is what our guide's love is – a prompt to the earthly self, which puts us back in touch with our soul's purpose in this lifetime at that particular moment in the meditation. We could imagine our guide saying during meditation, 'Look, this is how it feels to be really fearless', or 'This is what true clarity does for you. What gets in the way of you emulating these feelings in daily life at other times? Seek to let those earthly illusions go and these higher sensations and awarenesses will bring you, and all you are in touch with, great joy – and transform your world.'

And then, seeing the look on your face, he or she might say, 'Yes … well…. You may not be able to manage it all at once, but at least you know how it feels!'

A Way to Contact Your Guide

White Eagle was once asked, 'Is it advisable to get into contact with one's guide?' And he replied, in a way which helps us to further understand the delicacy of the relationship:

'It depends upon how you try to get into contact. It is not advisable to open the channel indiscriminately. Go into your inner sanctuary and ask your guide mentally or in your soul, "If it is good for me, good for others, that I should know you in full consciousness in this earthly life, will you make the effort to bring this knowledge to me?" If done thus, you may be sure that your guide will take the opportunity when it comes to make him- or herself known. In your innermost being, by your aspiration, and by development of a selfless spiritual consciousness, you will find you will meet your guide and teacher. In a remarkable way the guide will be made known to you.

'The great thing is to go quietly, humbly, trustingly. You will get the demonstration you seek most surely. There is someone with me now who is saying, "Tell them, 'To thine own self be true'". This is the secret. Be true to the highest that is within you, true to the spirit of brotherhood and love.'

23. Meeting our Master:
what is a Master Soul?

IN MEDITATION we can also find ourselves in the presence of what we might call a master. Bear in mind that master souls are beyond gender.

'Contact with those whom you call master is not often made on the astral plane, and there can be a misrepresentation of the masters from that plane. So it is necessary to train yourselves to become *en rapport* with the higher mental plane.… True meditation takes place on this plane.

'You will find your master on the ray most harmonious to yourself. He or she is part of you. You may hear and see him or her in some glorious sunset, or great piece of music, or in a lovely poem … in the message of a bed of flowers or in a pine tree.'

'The idea of meeting your master, whether in meditation or in earthly form, can be very appealing for a variety of reasons. The master meets a number of needs in us, from the most natural longing for a strong and loving father or mother figure, to the desire to be in the presence of and gain understanding and a broader perspective from a being who has trod this path before. Also, there can be an inner, almost subconscious need to be known, to be reminded of our spiritual nature and to copy what we see exemplified in the master. It is both understandable and to a degree essential that we seek a model for living as a spiritual being in a material world, since generally the world does not offer this. We need visions of what can be, what will be and what that beingness looks like.'

It is helpful to understand something of what mastery actually means. Mastery is control, in a positive sense: control of all the layers of one's being, to the point where even the death of the physical body can be overcome. The cells, the neural responses, all are under control. But this control only comes because we have mastered our responses both in thought and in feeling. That kind of mastery does not happen through the agency of anyone other than the self. No one can do it for us. We are in control of our own destiny in this sense. Every time we choose love we gain a little more control. One might say that we are internalizing our master. Surely this is what any master soul would wish for us? Not that we worship and revere them – they have no need for accolades and followers in that sense – but that we should join them in strength, wisdom and love.

Walking with your Master

Enter your meditation with the expectation that your master will join you and walk with you, even if you cannot see him or her. Trust is a crucial part of the meditative process.

Imagine what your master would look like: what they might be wearing, how they would deport themselves, the look in their eyes. Your master will have had many earthly lives and can appear in any one of a number of 'dresses'. Indeed it can be that he/she takes on a different 'dress' from the usual one from time to time, for the purpose of helping you.

You will, however, always recognize them from the particular aura they bring; the feeling you get when they are close by. Imagine that feeling now. Also remember that to reach mastery is to reach the place of spontaneous unconditional love. In other words, there will be no hint of chastisement or criticism or disapproval in your master's being, only complete respect and love and fellow-feeling.

Just as in physical life, it may help to imagine walking through a gateway into the garden of the spirit where you will meet your master. Perhaps just inside the gate you see footprints in the dew on the grass, leading off into the bliss of this perfect landscape. Walk in the footsteps of your master for a while, feeling in the soft turf the warmth beneath your bare feet.

These footsteps are leading you into the depths of the garden, but really this is an etheric metaphor for your consciousness being raised with each step. As you focus on where you place your feet, so the mind loses its business with outward things, and the love you feel for your master is drawing you onto a different level of awareness.

There will come a point when you will perceive, or feel, the master waiting for you, either to walk further side by side, or to sit together in communion heart to heart. This is a being who knows you, and has known you through many lifetimes, and who sees you deep down: not all the surface construction, which is still taking place, but the temple of your soul – which is being built through all the trials and mistakes of life. The master holds the vision of your perfection, and helps you to unveil it to yourself.

24. The Symbol, the Gesture, the Ritual

THE SIX-POINTED star, the hands together in prayer or *namaste*, lighting a candle – all these are aids to the mind and the earthly feelings, which prepare the self for meditation. The brain creates habits of thought and feeling around what keeps us safe and what is required for comfort, and symbols, gestures and ritual provide the brain with habits associated in meditation with upliftment.

When we repeat a gesture or a ritual or use a familiar symbol, the brain remembers the usual context of thought and feeling and we are switched into it almost automatically, and often without realizing it. This is what makes these aids work and why repetition of their use can be most helpful. For this reason, they are a support, but they are not the end in itself, of course, neither are they necessary to the extent that meditation cannot take place without them. To think thus is to confuse the object with its purpose. It also means that there can be a danger of being engrossed by the physicality of the symbol, gesture or ritual, rather than moving beyond it.

An example of this might come from any form of contact healing training, something we also take from White Eagle. There are rituals and gestures which need to be observed and learnt, but an obsession with getting these just right can impede the more important step, which is to surrender and be open to the flow of healing energy.

It is true, however, that some traditions see the actual

gestures, for example, as embodying the spiritual energy in and of themselves. This is true of *mudra*, the ritual gestures that are part of yoga and Buddhist technique, and used also in Jainism. One might say that our six-pointed star in the White Eagle Lodge is an example of this, being a representation of the Christ light so that it can be registered at an earthly level.

Using a focal image at the beginning of a meditation, something referred to in chapter twelve (p. 89) is one example of the use of a symbol, but there are also those symbols which appear spontaneously in meditation at the stage when one becomes etherically aware.

The Spirit Teaches the Body – Symbols in Meditation

'When men or women are searching for truth, when they have learnt to go to the very heart and centre of that truth, which is love, so that they themselves become love, they become tolerant. And when they become tolerant and humble, their inner vision opens and they learn to understand the symbols they see in meditation. The symbols speak to the person's soul; they convey truth to his or her soul. The person's spirit is teaching the soul. Have you ever thought of that? Your soul is a body, similar to your physical body, but it is built by your own thought, by your action and reaction. What you think, so you become. So the individual creates his or her soul body from the higher ether. Now it is through that soul body that the voice of spirit is heard. Spirit, which is the spark of God, the life of God, uses the soul body just as the soul body uses the physical body to contact physical things and physical life.'

The Star

'Usually it is thought that there are seven planes, but we would not limit the planes of your consciousness to seven. To illustrate, let us take the two-dimensional six-pointed star – at the moment the best symbol you have. Moreover, it is right to commence work on the two-dimensional symbol; but as the consciousness expands and the dimensions increase, that star which you see with but six points grows in life force, and develops eventually into a blazing star of one hundred and forty-four points. Then there should be suspended above your altar a blazing symbol of life force.

'As we meditate upon this star we find that from each of the countless points there issues a line of light and life. Now as that six-pointed star holds within its compass and can symbolize the countless points of life force, so also does the human being. In the beginning you are conscious only of one life – the physical body. Later, the five senses convey knowledge of a sixth sense which quickens the other five physical senses, enabling you to contact a form of life beyond or within the physical. Not only one form of life indeed, but plane upon plane, because from every one of the seven planes of consciousness in the human, from the physical to the highest, there issues a corresponding plane of inner consciousness. Thus we find there are seven times seven planes of life within man, and from these forty-nine planes, another forty-nine – and so forth, ever onward, until man comprehends all life, from the simplest to the greatest. Meditate on this, visualize your blazing star of one hundred and forty-four points, and the numberless rays of light streaming from every point.

'And what will you hear from the heart of your star? A voice: "I AM THAT I AM".'

The Winged Disc

The life cycle of the butterfly gives us a metaphor for the changes or metamorphosis that we go through, that state to which we are journeying through all the changes our lives bring. The transformation from the chrysalis is also one where we are free to fly. Of another symbol, White Eagle says:

'One of the symbols in use in the days of the Greek and Egyptian Masters was a great winged disc. You also have the symbol of the Sphinx with wings, the wings indicating the power of the soul to fly. There is no restriction on the human soul other than those it places upon itself. Therefore, think of having a pair of wings on your shoulders, of a winged disc, the latter being the symbol of the sun; and the sun, of course, being the Christ Spirit. All people are sons and daughters of God. *En masse* they are very young, only tiny sparks of God, but nevertheless all are children of God. The symbol of your heart centre is the golden sun, and the wings attached are the wings of your soul which, when you have learnt to use them, will enable you to fly into worlds supernal. You all have within you the power to do this.'

Ritual Sound

We explore chanting further in the next section, but when regarded in terms of ritual, chanting in meditation is an activity which is both physical and earthly, being part of a ritual, but is also an embodiment of spiritual energy when accompanied by thought, and this combination raises the consciousness.

'The spoken word creates a vibration or has the effect of a mantra and united to the innermost thought it is thereby enhanced. But words are useless without this inner force. The two together, perfectly spoken, will create double power and help.'

The Power of God is in Your Hands

Sit in a quiet space and think about your hands. Close your eyes and be aware of the physical hands in your lap, and turn the palms upwards. (If for some reason this is difficult, imagine your hands palm upwards in your lap.)

In the centre of each palm is a disc of light at the inner level. Picture this as if you were holding coins that are weightless, golden and radiant in each palm. These are the chakras of the hands, and they are linked with your heart.

With your eyes still closed, bring your hands up and together in *namaste*, the prayer position, in front of the centre of your chest, imagining those two circles joined and the power contained there, which is the power of the spirit. White Eagle says: 'The act of placing the hands together to form a triangle makes a focal point for the power'.

'Hands joined together ... the two hands, so significant – centres of power! What do they contain? They contain, first of all, the power to bless, the power to heal, the power to soothe the weary brow, the power to give.'

Feel that sense of the divine power of love opening your heart chakra and lifting your thoughts heaven-wards – raising your consciousness.

'Let us rest our hands in the hands of God, and know that God is good ...'

25. Harmonizing with the Divine

AS WAS MENTIONED in the previous section, there are reasons why we sometimes sound a mantra, which in White Eagle meditation is normally the AUM, before or during meditation. It is not absolutely necessary, but there are ways in which it can be helpful. The vibration of the AUM, as can be seen from the next teaching, creates a resonance in the body which attracts constructive vibrations. Thus chanting the AUM at the beginning of a meditation can help to penetrate the thought atmosphere around us, which then enables us to let go of the earthly mental preoccupations which can be so hard to release.

'The word 'mantras' is sometimes applied to certain sayings or writings contained in the Ancient Wisdom. On the inner planes, or esoterically, a mantra is a group of words arranged and used rhythmically to create certain vibrations – or, in other words, the bringing into manifestation of the unmanifested, through divine magic.

'In the beginning was the Word and the Word was with God, and the Word was God. We are taught that through the sounding of the sacred word of power, that which was before unmanifest came into manifestation on every plane of being. We are taught also that the sacred word, the innermost, is a creation of three sounds. Occultists speak of the great and beautiful name of "AUM", which word you have heard us use. Divide the word in three – "A" - "U" - "M" – and we are coming nearer to the sound of vibration which first brought manifestation into being. These three letters or sounds are found represented in all the ancient religions; according to the interpretation of the particular race, these three are found. But by "sound" let us not assume only the vibration on the outer plane of human speech, but that which vibrates through creation as a result of being ... do you follow? ... the actual soul-note of creation.'

'*In the beginning was the Word; and the Word was with God; and the Word was God.* From the beginning, then, came the Word. The Word is the centre. The Word of God, the Name of God, is the dot within the circle; and from the Word, from God, everything in life proceeds. So soon as human being can draw close again to the Word of God and touch that creative centre, he or she becomes attuned to all life, and enters into a state of at-one-ment, which is the goal, the apex, of life.'

'God spoke the Word. God breathed forth the life and it spread over the whole earth. As life spread and got further away from its centre, it became more chaotic; it lost touch with its centre, except on certain occasions – that is to say when the holy, sacred Word of Power was sounded. But how are you able in your difficult life to get back to attunement? The Word is sounded not by word of mouth, but by the thought, the prayer if you like, by the aspiration to the Godhead. In your meditation you strive to touch that place of stillness, that silence beneath life. You sound in your souls one of the names of God, the great "AUM," and as that mantra is chanted with your heart, with your love and aspiration, you create this vibration.

'You see: your actions, your whole life, makes a vibration or a sound. Every individual soul is therefore sounding a note, a vibration. When the harmonious and right vibration goes forth from you, it finds its exact mark, and so it will return. As you sound, so you will receive – this is cause and effect. This happens on all planes. Spiritually, when you send out that note of Christ love, you naturally absorb into yourself harmony, peace of mind, all things which create in your environment harmony and progress. It is an exact law.'

Harmonizing with the Divine

As you sit quietly in preparation for meditation, imagine you are listening to the AUM being chanted in the distance and gradually drawing closer to you. You hear the distinct sounds of the chant, A... U... MMMMM.

As you imagine this chant, think of it as sounding the highest love you can conceive; a power so great that it is beyond earthly things, and yet it is something which your deepest heart recognizes as being the source of your life.

Take a few 'straw breaths' (see p. 40) and when you are ready, join in with the chant you 'hear' in your mind, while focusing in your mind and heart on the Divine Source.

Feel your whole being responding to that sound, which vibrates in every cell of your body and in all your auras. (Try not to judge the quality of the sound with the earthly mind – in spirit it will be heard as a perfect expression of your heart.)

Repeat the AUM for as long as you wish. If you are doing it yourself, it is all on one note, projected forth, the vowel changing without a new breath each time. It can be a meditation in itself, or lead into a deep silence, or an opening of the inner vision – it will bring whatever is your soul's need for your individual self at this moment.

Sounding the Word

'Listen, when you are in the country, and if you can silence the lower or objective senses and open the inner hearing – and – Oh! supreme experience! – hear the Great Word, AAAAUUUMMMM ... AAAAUUUMMMM, pervade all things.... God's Voice, the voice of the cosmic body.'

'AUM.... Beloved brethren, we sound the word of God in your being. If you cannot utter it with a sound on earth, then do it mentally many times in your waking moments. When you do this something is happening to your soul and to your body. It does not happen immediately but long continued practice of the AUM, not only the sound of the AUM, not only the mental vibration of the AUM, but the spiritual activity of the AUM in your own individual universe, is creating for you a new body, a new being. It is the word of creation, the magic word.'

Chanting the AUM

White Eagle is very clear that it is important to be in a place where you will not be disturbed in order to chant the AUM (OM) safely. This is because of the power that chanting this word from the heart can have on the chakras, on the etheric body and on the mind.

Before beginning your chanting, attune yourself to selfless love as White Eagle describes it:

'As you become attuned to a beautiful vibration through that selfless love, you will hear within yourself, so that the self within becomes a part of the greater self, of the universal self, the God life, the life spirit of the universe. You will then hear the great word … the AUM. A…U…M. Hear the pulsating word, life-giving, healing, raising you into the spheres of light.'

You raise your consciousness to become attuned in this way through your compassion for people, animals, the Earth herself, or your love for God. Allow your feelings to be moved beyond earthly emotion to the place of deep devotion and divine understanding. As you attune to divine love, so you will be in the right frame of mind to approach your chanting.

The sound is a triple one – made up of three separate 'seed' syllables, so that A … U … and M… are given equal weight and time on each breath. They sound like OM when they are sung together. Yet this is not as important as where your inward focus lies.

If it helps, you could imagine being part of a circle of monks, who are all chanting with you. Imagine that the sound you make is coming from the spiritual self within. It is not dependent on whether you think you can sing, whether you have chanted before, or how you make the sound. It is your own higher truth, and no matter how it outwardly sounds, it is a free, pure and beautiful spiritual vibration from your heart, which allows the angels of creativity and healing to draw close.

When you finish chanting – the number of times is up to how you feel – allow the silence to grow for a while, so that the inner vibration of creative life which the sounds convey can continue to be felt in every cell of your body, in every part of your being.

26. The Smile of the Buddha

SOME OF US will be familiar with lives spent as Buddhist monks, whether we are now in a man's or a woman's body. We may have far memories either consciously remembered, or unconsciously present in our soul. In meditation we can connect with those memories, or with the essence of what the Buddhist awareness brings us. White Eagle himself said when referring to his work through his medium: '... we would explain to you all that we do not work on the purely mental or mind plane when we come, but on the intuitional or Buddhic* plane of consciousness'. He refers to this plane of consciousness (the closeness of the word to 'Buddha' is mere coincidence) a number of times, linking it with the intuition, and describes to us the particular quality present:

'Those of you who practise meditation will know that when the object of your meditation is the Lord Buddha, you find yourself before his gracious silent presence, which is pervaded by a peace and stillness almost beyond comprehension. The tendency, when you come into the thought-field of the Buddha, is to slow down all mental activity, and to arrive at the centre of silence. Compare this path with our present method of entering into meditation or contemplation. You know that the whole ritual of meditation is to silence all sound in yourself. While it is impossible to silence your environment in a town, you can train yourself

*The Buddhic plane is a plane of enlightenment, not the plane of the Buddha

so that quietness rules in your physical, in your mental, in your emotional and astral body. You can so rule your magnetic field that you come to a place of complete and utter stillness.

'Why do you do this? Because it is necessary to quieten the outer life in order to become aware of the jewel within the lotus – this jewel being the divine spark, the divine consciousness within the innermost being of every individual. Those people who are most active in the flesh and in the mind live in a mental world of turbulence, and are unable to hear God's voice.

'To go back to the Lord Buddha, to the teaching of the silence and the inner sanctuary of stillness: it is there that we shall find and comprehend the meaning of love. In the silence we can know the glory and the ecstasy of love which leads to reunion with God.'

There is much about images of the Buddha that can help us in our meditation practice. The uprightness of the spine, balanced on a wide contact with the earth in the lotus position, gives us the sensation of being balanced between heaven and earth, part of life and yet connected to heaven, and with the crown chakra open. So too the chest area of the Buddha is open and lifted; the heart is open to the sun and lifted in acknowledgement of all beings, rather than closed in upon itself.

And then there is the smile on the faces of many of the statues of the Buddha, particularly those from Thailand. That smile is gentle, relaxed and enigmatic, as if the Buddha is saying, in White Eagle's words, 'All is well'. The smile is from a being which sees beyond the limitations of the earth existence, into the world of illumination and ultimate bliss, yet holds compassionately to the suffering of

earthly beings with a great radiation of love and understanding.

Dispassion

One of the qualities which the Buddhic plane reveals is
that of dispassion. White Eagle links this with the symbol
of the lotus which is familiar to many who meditate, both
as a starting point, but also as an image which can appear
at certain times to guide the meditator. As we read what
White Eagle says about dispassion, we can see how this
arises from our practice of stillness and becomes fundamental to the growth of the soul which meditation on the
white lotus can enable:

'Will you visualize the form of the white lotus? Let us
see this flower as resting upon the surface of the stilled
waters, its roots reaching down into the mud beneath. Let
us see in this symbol a deep truth, as representative of the
soul which has become at peace, that is stilled, untouched
by the storms and passions of life … the soul which has
learned the lesson of dispassion. We think this lesson of
dispassion to be one of the most important lessons which
the candidate treading the path towards the major initiations must learn.

'We recognize the sensitiveness which results from the
increase of the spiritual forces within, which latter are as-
sisted in their growth by the great rays of light and power
from on high. But he who would become worthy of initiation into the temple of the holy mysteries must learn
dispassion … must learn to be unaffected, undisturbed, by
those things which usually cause the less understanding, or
younger brother, to fly into a state of mind which must cut

him off from those spiritual blessings of God which indeed are his birthright.

'The symbol of the (lotus) should bring to our waiting minds this state of dispassion which we seek. It is a symbol of annunciation … of initiation. It tells those who are the silent watchers of human growth and spiritual unfoldment when the soul is ready to be guided towards the gates of heaven. It is a symbol of impersonal service. The rose symbolizes human and divine love, and in the life of the Christ man or woman we see this complete blending. The lotus also represents this love, but a universal love, a love withdrawn from the personal. It is a complete symbol of life. We see represented in this form the six-pointed star, within the centre of which dwells the life of God … the central point within the six-pointed star … which stands as the complete symbol of the God life: star of brotherhood, of power and wisdom. We would suggest then, that the lotus is a symbol of power.'

Meditation for Dispassion

You are met in the garden by a seated figure. A Buddhist monk sitting simply on the grass. He looks up and smiles, and this is an invitation for you to sit with him. You sit opposite him and see that in his hands he holds a simple white lotus bloom, which you contemplate with him in the silence. After a while he puts the lotus down on a small pool which appears between you, and then raindrops begin to fall, dappling the surface of the pool. You sit on in silence and stillness, and he teaches you the lesson of non-resistance and equanimity in the face of all. Your attention may be drawn outwards to the sounds around you, and the sensations and thoughts of the body, but you feel you could experience the stillness and silence underneath any noise, or sensation.

In that silence you may experience your true self, free from limitation. You may feel greater, more aware on many levels. As you return to complete earthly consciousness, you earth this awareness and this ability to be more than you think you are. White Eagle says:

'With the union, the mystical marriage, between the human soul and the Christ Spirit, we see a wonderful picture, a lotus flower held by invisible hands in the highest heavens. The lotus flower is the chakra of the heart of the individual and of all humanity. The lotus flower is held high in this mystical, golden radiance, and gently opens its petals. Above this bowl, this lotus flower, shines the Son, the Cosmic Christ, the beginning and the end. This is life eternal, your life.'

The Lotus of the Self

The lotus is symbolic of the heart chakra, but we can also see it as a representation of our whole self.

The roots reach down into the rich earth of human experience. The stem is surrounded by the water of our emotional responses to what we encounter in daily life. The flower holds itself above these waters in pure air with focused purpose, and then opens to the fire of the sun, the light, the warmth and God's love.

All the elements are represented here: earth, water, air,

fire. White Eagle does not say that ether is separate from these, but rather that there is an etheric counterpart to earth, water, air and fire. It is the etheric which links us with our soul and spirit. So the most perfect expression of all these elements will produce, eventually, the fully-evolved flower of the God self.

The earth brings to our roots nourishment and steadiness. It brings us the opportunities to make choices. The water brings us the chance to develop poise amid the changing circumstances of life, and for the lotus to grow the water needs to be still. The air brings clarity, it allows the light through; the air needs to be pure in order to offer a lucid focus for the sun's rays. The fire of the sun draws forth our own warmth and love.

The pattern of growth is also important. We have to learn all about the earth, otherwise we would not be grounded and receptive. The stem grows strong through this to withstand any buffeting of the waters flowing around us. But once that bud reaches the air it does not rest on the surface of the water, but lifts itself above the emotional state into a realm of purity of mind, where it can open unimpeded and fully to the Sun.

Moreover, what actually causes the lotus to grow? White Eagle says we contain the seed atom of God within us, which is the Christ child, a reflection of God's light. The warmth of the sun sets up a resonance which is felt within every cell of the body or of the plant or of us, and calls forth that seed atom to arise and grow towards the Light. That arisen self is the Christ within, called forth by the Father (Sun); and it is nurtured and given what it needs to grow by the Mother (Earth).

27. In the Aura of the Angels

THE ANGELIC level of reality is manifestly different from ours. We could say that it is closer to heaven. We recognize it through its distinct quality of stillness – a stillness which is not simply devoid of movement, but detached from thought and feeling. It is akin to sensory deprivation but without any fear or negativity attached; it is pure awareness, rather than being connected with any sensation.

To find our way to this level is to experience the deepest peace possible while in a physical form and to receive profound healing through that peace, which is of mind and emotion, as well as of the body.

The mind seems to float, not in a cloud of dull, sleepy or drug-induced stupor, but rather in a bright clarity existing outside the need to think. The emotions are quiescent, not through suppression, but through being in harmony with the divine purpose of life.

The angelic level is open to those who can find stillness, and who believe in the angels and acknowledge them.

Meditation Leading to the Angelic Sphere

Make yourself sufficiently comfortable in your chair that you will not need to move later; upright and with cushions behind the back if needed. This comfort is vital so that all movement in the body can cease, then the physical nervous system relaxes and the etheric takes over.

Deliberately relax your muscles, especially those of the shoulders and the neck, keeping the spine lifted and the chest open if you can, or have that in your mind as a vision of perfection. Images or statues of Thai or other Buddhas should give you the position to emulate.

As you become more still, allow your mind to believe that you can and are entering the aura of the angels. Ask your own angel to guide you if you wish. That guidance will take the form of an enveloping, deepening quietude.

You may not see anything, and it is best not to expect to see, because the mind will get busy with form. Rather, experience with your whole being a sense of being held in space and time, cocooned, centred in the core of beingness, without being anything specific.

If you think of anything, think of being aware and being all.

No matter whether you are aware of this or not, the angelic level of consciousness will have been reached through the profundity of your stillness and acknowledgment of the existence of another level of reality. This is the handle of the door, which is on our side – a favourite White Eagle saying.

28. Earthing Heaven

IN ORDER for us really to make use of this book, there has to be a way in which we can bring the experience gained in meditation through into our daily lives. We know, from what White Eagle assures us of, that the soul has grown during meditation, no matter what we may have experienced mentally, and that the etheric link between our physical body and its etheric counterpart and our eternal soul is strengthened. However, we are here on earth for a purpose and so putting our meditations to use is important – as White Eagle says:

'The purpose of physical life is that you may bring through into manifestation, through the physical, that greater consciousness of the inner life, or the God life. The limitations of the physical are the necessary test. In this way humanity's – shall we call it 'efficiency', or its power? – to bring through the inner life to the outer, is tested. We may experience full illumination in a higher state of consciousness, but this will happen while still in the physical body. The physical body is as much part of God as the spirit: "as above, so below".

'There cannot be separation, and that is the whole point – the complete interpenetration of all these planes. God is as much in your physical body as in your higher spiritual consciousness, and though you may experience that illumination out of the body, you must be able to express it and live it, in the body.'

Bringing it Back; Feeling the Vibrational Change

One way to earth the vibrations experienced in meditation is simply to acknowledge the changes in ourselves as we return. As we are breathing our way back, becoming aware of our body again and of the physical senses, we can pause and reflect on the difference in our feelings or thoughts, as well as the sensation of peace, stillness, or strength in our body. The more we are aware of the subtle changes, the more we will recognize them – the brain gets used to identifying them and realizing their importance. That in turn can mean that when we return to meditation again we will quite possibly have a deeper experience.

Earthing Love

There are ways in which the feelings experienced in meditation can be so profound and moving that it is hard to feel connected with the outer world again, especially if one's circumstances are currently challenging. One way to overcome any resistance and feeling of disillusionment with our life as we return is to think with love of all that is around us, no matter how difficult those things might be. Any true connection in meditation is with the higher planes, with heaven, and as such with divine love. Therefore, the channel for love will be wider; the heart will be more open and receptive, so it is an ideal time to try to bring through that love into our lives.

'So, live that you are not always thinking of foolish and trivial things; do not fill the mind of the head with a lot of trash but let it be usefully engaged. When you sit at home quietly, let your heart meditate upon beautiful and joyous and helpful things. For instance, 'how can I best serve my brothe, my sister?' By understanding them, by helping them, by being kind and thoughtful, by being on the lookout for little ways in which I can be courteous and kindly. This mind in the heart must become active, glorifying God.'

Making it Real, Putting it out There, Using it

'Let us now meditate together on the at-one-ment of life. In your meditation try to realize that you are not separate but that you all are of the one spirit. You have to learn that humanity is one vast brotherhood of life; that all nature is part of you; you are part of nature; you are part of the animal kingdom; you are part of the air and the birds in the air and the fish in the sea; you are part of the whole of creation, because you are a part of God and all creation is in God.

'To reach this realization, you must rise in your imagination into the golden light, the supreme light, and there prostrate yourselves humbly before the Almighty: God, in Whom we all live and breathe … Who is Infinity and Eternity…. It is impossible for the spirit to be separated from itself. All are in IT. You can never lose a loved one, for that loved one is with you, an individual close to you. Listen to his or her voice speaking to you in the language of the spirit, which is love … and *love* and *love*. You cannot be separated from anyone you love either on this earth or in the soul world. Think often along these lines and let the soul or spirit world become part of this physical world for you.'

Where is Heaven on Earth?

'Do not set material things before the God things. *Seek ye first the kingdom of God.* Let that be still the desire of your life, your first aspiration as you wake in the morning: to seek God and all the beauty of God's world. Then you will be living with a purpose. Then you will be making great strides on the path of spiritual evolution, and your goal – as we have already said – is complete union with the holy, infinite life; at-one-ment with the Father. Always you will be yourself because God has endowed you with personal life, but your bliss will only come when you recognize your at-one-ment with the whole, and when you are able to participate in the communion of saints.'

'This is the secret: to live, to know and to be, to be in the consciousness of the Infinite Love and Light, and to live for spirit and not for matter. Matter is secondary; spirit is the first and foremost, and to live rightly you must live to develop the consciousness of the Great White Light or the Christ within yourself. Not here, in the brow, my friends, but [*pointing*] here in the heart, and in the thousand-petalled lotus at the apex of your triangle.'

White Eagle was once asked: 'Is it possible to remain aware of this higher consciousness all through the working day?' His reply was:

'It is possible but difficult. It comes with continual aspiration and self-discipline. As you progress on the path of continual meditation you get two levels of consciousness – that is to say, you may be engaged in everyday things on the surface, but beneath the surface there is always this consciousness of the universal divine love. You become aware beneath the daily consciousness all the time. It depends upon the level, the particular state that the soul has reached. Not all souls can feel this. You must not forget the help that is always yours when you discipline yourself to the life of gentleness, selflessness and purity. Pure souls in your spiritual environment will aid and guide and help you through every problem and difficulty. Every material problem can be solved, for love is the great solvent – without fail. Without hesitation, we would add, to those of you who are seeking spiritual unfoldment, spiritual knowledge, and understanding of the higher spheres of life – meditation is the path which must be pursued.'

About the Appendices

APPENDIX ONE contains a 'path' of meditation such as White Eagle suggests, for readers: an eight-week programme of exercises, designed to support the practice. It's hoped that through undertaking this programme, you will, if you wish, become so used to such a path that you carry on with it – creating your own sequence, adapting the exercises to suit you, deepening your awareness, and finding your heaven, not only within, but throughout your life.

You will recognize some of the exercises from the main text, but some are new. Where we have repeated text from the chapters this is for your convenience, to save you looking back.

Appendix Two offers specific focus on some of the difficulties you may encounter, and Appendix Three is a kind of glossary or checklist of the characteristics of White Eagle meditation.

The Daily Practice

In the sequence that follows (Appendix One), the focus of the practice will each day be on a particular aspect of the meditation process, rather than a full meditation. The purpose of this is to set up a regular daily routine which you feel able to stick to. To sit with the intention to meditate can be inhibiting, rather like looking at a blank canvas is for the artist, but to follow a simple and short routine which carries no expectations with it builds confidence and develops tenacity. Nonetheless the hope is that with this practice the etheric bridge, as White Eagle calls it, is intensified – so that the love, power and wisdom of the greater self can flow towards us, and we are able to develop our inner senses. Consequently, without our holding expectations, longer and deeper meditation can happen from time to time. The secret is not to anticipate it!

The sequence will be the same each day, but the practice will vary day by day and week by week, so that you gain experience in the variety of elements of meditation. This also means that the meditative exercise is always creative and fresh and doesn't become monotonous, something which can lead to the mind wandering. At the same time there will be elements which work for you, but not necessarily for someone else, and from those you can then structure your own meditation so that it is suitable for your needs.

Having a regular ritualized practice which we do not deviate from, but which is nevertheless creative, helps to develop our confidence in meditating and our inner awareness. You will begin to be surprised by the reality of heaven!

The suggested sequence to follow each morning is to:

- Sit or lie and take a few conscious breaths
- Focus on stillness
- Do whatever is the practice for the day (see below)
- Earth the vibrations
- Use a simple sealing ritual, or a fuller ritual if a meditation has occurred

The programme set out here lasts for eight weeks, after which it can be repeated, or from it you can then create your own structured meditation, bearing in mind what is said in chapter 3, 'Trusting the Process of Meditation', and by using any elements from this book.

Not all the processes given in this appendix are to be found in the book. Some are adapted, some created specially. Neither have all the exercises in the book been used here, so you may find others that appeal to you more when you come to create your ritual.

Reflection Days

The seventh day of the week is a reflection day. On each seventh day we invite you to contemplate the week's meditative activities. As part of that reflection, consider if there is anything you feel you could apply to your daily life. Perhaps something was particularly powerful or meaningful. Maybe there was growth of understanding which you feel would help in your everyday life. The point then is that the seventh day becomes in itself an earthing of that particular feeling, thought, or practice.

It may be easily forgotten as the day progresses, so you could use an affirmation as a memory aid, or carry any kind of *aide memoire* which will bring the understanding back into focus during the day, and enable you to earth that particular vibration of heaven. In White Eagle's words one is putting into practice the divine law: 'As above, so below'.

Appendix One

Week One, Day 1: Being Still

At the Heart of the Breath

Sit comfortably and as upright as you can. If it feels comfortable, fold your hands one in front of the other in your lap close to your body, which means your thumbs are what you see when you look down. This is a natural position for the bones of the arms and wrists, which allows the elbows to relax down by your sides and importantly the tops of the shoulders can relax. The crucial thing, though, is that you feel comfortable, so adjust until you do. Remember that you are seeking to allow the physical nervous system to let go, so that eventually the etheric counterpart can take over.

Close your eyes and turn your inner gaze down, without dropping your chin. Feel the cheeks and tongue and brow spreading out to the sides.

Now the only movement you may be aware of is your breathing. Just watch the breath, without interfering with it. Feel how it moves your ribs and chest muscles, as the lungs expand and then release. Follow the movement inwardly. Bring all your focus to that feeling. As you bring all your attention to this one movement, so the rest of your body becomes more and more still. It is as if all your energies were focused on this one activity.

This rhythm is the constant in your life and will be happening whether you are aware of it or not – the breath not only of earth, but the divine energies, flowing and sustaining you. So now take your attention away from the movement and instead feel the quality of stillness you have generated within. Immerse your mind in your body's stillness; be aware of its qualities – how it feels.

If something external, or another thought, grabs your attention, see it as the flotsam on the top of the waves, while you rest in the deep, peaceful blue underneath. Part of you will be aware of the disturbance, but you remain still at the heart of the breath. If you need a focus, come back to watching the breath again, and after a while again let it go, and feel the stillness again.

Week One, Day 2: Resting Upright

The Spine as a Rod of Light

Sit upright, draw yourself erect and feel what happens within your body when you do this. The physical spine is curved, but the inner 'rod of light' of the spine, which is the linking channel of energy between all the chakras, is like a plumbline.

Drop your shoulders and the lobes of your ears. Lift the heart and the crown in your mind, without physically lifting.

Use your will to visualize your inner spine as a rod of light which is balanced between heaven and earth, so it reaches right down into the earth through the hips and upwards beyond the crown of the head, with your self at the centre.

Now feel that you are drawing all your energies into the centre to be around the focus of the inner spine – to identify with the central poise of the spirit. It may be that you sense you are slightly off-centre in one part; perhaps you sway very slightly this way and that until your spine feels aligned with the spiritual forces. You may do this physically, but then imagine the inner adjustments and alignment which are happening. Keep focusing on this sense of getting closer and closer to perfect alignment.

As you do this you will find you become more and more still and silent within; more and more lifted in all ways. Feel what happens, and the sensations which come to you. This is the true sense of poise. Feel what it feels like. Become familiar with the sensation of poise and stillness.

Be aware of this feeling, trying to be completely still and have the thought that just as your body and mind come into that poised space, so your aspirations can become lifted towards God – a sense of moving upwards, without effort into the spiritual state.

You are linked with the spirit through this 'rod of light'; you are held safely and without effort in a state of poised receptivity. As you remain in this position, just being aware of this line of inner light, with all else dropping, relaxing away from it, so the inner will of your spirit takes over. You have created the condition for this to happen and from here your meditation can unfold. However, even if you just stay with that feeling of deepest stillness and poise, you will find it is powerful in itself as a means of bringing strength and the courage to will the Will of God in your life.

Week One, Day 3: Focus

The Golden Light of the Spiritual Sun

Sit with your hands palms upwards in your lap and close your eyes. With every in-breath imagine that every cell of the body, particularly in the upturned palms of the hands and the crown of the head, is taking in the light – in this case a warm, comforting, golden light.

There is no sense of strain, just that every part of you is

like a magnet for that light to enter, and flood the whole body with golden light.

And then with every outbreath, put your attention on the heart chakra at the centre of your chest and feel that golden light is radiating there.

As the breath goes out the golden radiance spreads and fills the chest and gradually beyond. Feel the spreading and opening of the physical chest, and imagine how at the etheric level that golden light is radiating in the expanding heart chakra.

Again there is no strain to push out the light, or to think of where it might be going, just a focus on receiving and then expanding in radiance.

So the limited mind is focused on breathing, on the surface of the skin, and then on the heart…nothing more. The gold colour of the light brings warmth and strength, also a feeling of safety…of being held in a powerful and reassuring protection much more than the mind of earth can provide.

Week One, Day 4: Rising

Above the Clouds

If you have ever been in a plane, you may have experienced that moment when it rises up above the clouds, and you are in the sunlight again. Close your eyes and imagine that sensation of coming out above dark, heavy clouds into the light of the sun. Feel the lightness in as many ways as you can….

Feel the sun's rays penetrating every part of your body, the spiritual sunlight of God, as well as earthly warmth. Feel the relaxation of the body – letting tension dissipate, the muscles relaxing, the smile of summer sunlight filling your heart and mind.

We can practise the ability to rise above the heaviness of earth into the sunlight and sometimes repeating an affirmation can help. Choose one of these that fits you, and repeat it inwardly whenever you feel the need, remembering the warmth, lightness and light of the spiritual Sun, and the power of the Sun of God available within your heart.

I can rise above this; I can lift off above all the heaviness of earth.
I can get above the turbulent emotions and the worrying mind.
I can find warmth, strength and peace above the mind and feelings.

Week One, Day 5: Experiencing

The Transforming Archway of Light

You are standing before an archway filled with light. Through this archway is the positive sphere of heaven, and this entrance is a transforming portal. This means that as you step into it what we call negative states of mind and feeling are transmuted into their opposite: dullness of mind becomes clarity, heaviness of body becomes lightness and freedom of movement, and sadness and depression become joy.

Stand in the archway and feel the light flowing down, over and through your whole being. Allow the transformation to take place, as a butterfly accepts the shedding of its chrysalis – so that when you step forwards through the portal and out into the sunlight, you can recognize how different you are feeling.

Week One, Day 6: Radiating

Star Radiation

Visualize a sun, or a six-pointed star if you can. As in the exercise on day 3, feel that sun or star at the centre of your chest. Etherically this is the heart chakra – the seat of divine love – and it will begin to open.

Love cannot hold to itself; its nature is to flow outwards to all life, to radiate. So as you breathe, imagine the sun or star pouring out light in all directions from your heart centre. This light is divine love and is the creative power which can transform all that it touches. Don't think of where it is going, or to whom, just focus on the radiation of that powerful light as a vibration which transcends all earthly impediments, and changes lives.

Week One, Day 7: Reflection Day

Week Two, Day 1: Flowing

Circulating Life-Force

Sit quietly and close your eyes, laying your hands palm upwards one on each thigh. Breathe gently and without effort, noticing the sensations as you breathe: the lungs pushing the ribs out at the sides; the coolness in the nostrils as you breathe in; the relaxing of the chest as you breathe out.

Imagine you are seated in a pool of light, which shines all around you, and even through you, like a magical, but harmless ray in a science fiction story. This light is not only harmless, but full of health, well-being, comfort.

Focus on your breath again, and imagine that it is the means by which this light can flow into you. Imagine it flowing in through your left foot and left hand; travelling up through and around your head, and down and out through the right hand and foot. Be aware of this 'circulating light stream' with every breath you take. You don't have to breathe deeply, or change the rhythm of your breath at all; it simply happens, and will go on happening, even when your mind is elsewhere.

Feel that this 'stream of light' is being absorbed into every cell as you breathe in, and as you breathe out, it flows from you in a vibration of love towards all life.

After a few moments take your thoughts away from your breathing, and become aware of the outer world again – your body on the chair; the sounds around you. When you open your eyes wait for a while and know that this vivifying life-stream is constantly flowing in you; that your conscious awareness of it for this short while has cleared the channels and enhanced the flow of this Christ light.

Week Two, Day 2: Letting Go

The Secret and Power of Letting Go and Letting God

Imagine as you sit ready to meditate that you could hear God speaking, or a master saying to you: 'Let go and let me take care of it all.' And by 'all', you know he or she means not just taking care of your life and health, but that of your friends, the animal kingdom, other peoples and the world. In fact, all the things you are anxious about; all the things which worry you, make you tense or angry or feel powerless. Just imagine it now.

Close your eyes and feel the presence with you, the presence that can do anything, and which knows everything and how everything fits together in the grand scheme and throughout time. Feel that that presence also knows every hair of your head and therefore you have nothing to be anxious about, even when it seems you do from an earthly perspective – all is taken care of and all will be well. So even if you can't quite believe it, imagine how it might feel to hear those words, feel that reassurance, support, care and underlying strength.

Now feel how your shoulders relax and your eyes relax. You find you take a deeper breath on a sigh of release – and you surrender into that care. That is the beginning of your meditation.

Whenever you feel agitated, or not 'getting there' during the meditation, come back to that thought and feeling; if you manage just that, you will be healing every part of yourself, and as well as raising your vibrations.

Week Two, Day 3: Imagining

Painting with the Mind

Sit or lie comfortably. You are an artist, able to work in more than three dimensions, able to create anything from any angle you wish.

This time, create a still pool in front of you – blue, clear, shining. Go down under the water in thought, and create a lotus bud resting in the mud. Draw it with your mind – a bud on a stem, which you lengthen upwards towards the surface of the water. Extend the stem, waving slightly up until the tip of the lotus bud touches the surface. Draw the slight ripple as it breaks the surface.

Time elapses, and now you draw the stem as it reaches up in the light of the sun and you create the bud beginning to open. You may find you draw the leaves spreading out on the surface – their lovely curving shapes – and then focus again on drawing the lotus petals opening, until you create the open flower, cupping the stamens. Lotuses can be many different colours. Paint yours to suit your mood, include the colour of the centre.

Why stop there?! Create the perfume of the lotus. Create the smoothness of the petals. Create the feeling you receive as you gaze at its heart.

Week Two, Day 4: Contemplating the Highest

The God within, and within which we Live

If you were asked, 'What is the God within your own being?' how would you reply?

Take a moment now and close your eyes and let that question rest in your mind without resistance to it. Breathe your resistance away and be open to whatever emerges. How does God within manifest?

No matter what is happening, all around you and within you is an intelligent, loving presence which knows how things are and what soul choices have been made … an all-powerful presence which holds you and upholds you through all things.

Close your eyes again and take your attention to the flow of the life force within you as you breathe. Feel that you sit at the centre of a sphere of consciousness, and that consciousness flows all around you and through you. It doesn't matter what it looks like; just imagine it is there, and if you imagine it as light, energy, divine essence, colour, peace, joy, or simply breath, that is fine … whatever comes to you is how it is for you…. All that is required is that you keep bringing your thoughts back to this awareness, which may change as the seconds pass.

At this moment you are aware of how God, the light, the divine consciousness, is the motivating and life-giving essence of your life. It is not something separate from you, or a distant goal, and it is in all life and links you with all life.

This awareness could lead to any kind of meditation, so just go with what works for you, but if you wish, expand your thoughts into the space around you physically, feeling this connection with everything as the life force flows through all, and then include what you wouldn't perceive with physical senses…. What are you connected with at a subtle, spiritual level?

Week Two, Day 5: Meeting

Imagining your own Heaven

First, think about the kind of environment which makes you feel in touch with spiritual things: is it among trees, in a temple, a small chapel, mountains, a garden?

Create a place like this in your mind, a place in the etheric where, at this moment, you feel you would be most able to be at one with your spirit.

Find a spot there where you can lie or sit, kneel, or stand and open wide your arms and your heart to your greatest self – to your spiritual essence.

Imagine the greater part of your soul existing in that place, and the positive energies flowing to you in your physical body and personality.

What would you most want to learn from your spirit? Imagine that happening, and what would be said.

Whatever your need at this moment, allow yourself to receive it from heaven – the most exact and effective transforming or sustaining power.

Week Two, Day 6: Heart Mind

Meditation on 'the Point of Union between the Heart and the Higher Mind'

Visualize the heart centre as aflame with love, visualizing a flame perhaps within a lotus or a rose... the tip of the flame is reaching up to the brow; to the mind...

Have the feeling that the ordinary mind of everyday is opening, letting go, becoming still so that the warmth of the flame can awaken the higher mind – the inner will and wisdom... .

The heart's light and the mind's light merge ... and reach up through the crown... .

The flame from the heart warms and brightens the mind, dissolving narrow, dark thoughts and expanding the consciousness....

The vision opens to perceive and become aware of heavenly things....

Week Two, Day 7: Reflection Day

Week Three, Day 1:
No Expectations

In the Waiting Room

Waiting rooms are full of expectations. Imagine yourself sitting in a waiting room on the outskirts of heaven. Beyond the archway you can see a beautiful garden. Occasionally the scents of the flowers waft into the room, with the sounds of laughter. You long to have the power to go through the arch, but you feel feeble. You imagine what you will find there – the greatest longings of your heart at this moment being the connection with God.

You look up at a sign on the wall in front of you that says: 'The secret of strength lies in the quiet mind'. Something clicks – if you wish to find the ability to transcend the heaviness of earth, you realize, you have to let go of all desire, all expectations of yourself and of what you will find.

You close your eyes to the room and the heavenly garden. You imagine yourself as a grail cup – the mind and feelings quite clear of all longing, just resting completely contentedly in this moment, just as you are. If there are thoughts in your mind about your ability, or anything which gets in the way of simply being, see those thoughts flowing out of your cup as you breathe out, until it is empty.

Simply be, and in that moment of acceptance you will be aware that God – all strength, wisdom and love – is within. You'll know that what appears to be empty is full of light!

Week Three, Day 2: Centring

Sensing More

Feel every single place through which your body touches the earth. Feel your hips on the chair, or your back on the bed. Feel your hands in your lap and the sensation of the texture of your clothing. Feel your feet touching the floor. Feel the skin of your face and neck, and be aware of the air touching the skin. Scan the whole surface of the body for every place where there is sensation – the physical nerves passing messages to the brain – this is hot, this is cold, this is hard, this is soft.

Then go inwards and try to be aware of the sensations inside your body. Inside your head, behind your eyes, in your mouth and nose, the muscles of your neck and back, and deeper still – the breath moving the chest, the feelings in the belly. Scan the inside of your body for every place where you are aware of feeling.

You may be aware of your heartbeat on the left, but now come to your heart chakra at the centre of your chest, something beyond just the physical sensation. Focus on that point, a sensation of expansion in love. Be aware of all awareness coming into that one place, which is a portal: a giving and receiving centre.

Week Three, Day 3: Being Aware

Realizing and Creating Beauty: Meditative Exercise

Sit quietly and think of the things in life which you find beautiful. Imagine the most beautiful colours, scenery, music, form. Notice how these things are not necessarily known as beautiful by the world, but are the things you love.

If you had to choose a flower or a tree to represent beauty, what would you choose? With your eyes closed, picture this flower or tree as clearly as you can, but in bud against a grey sky, or as a young sapling just pushing up from the dark earth.

There may be a part of your life which feels ugly, or even a part of yourself. Acknowledge this, but then place that symbol of beauty – the bud of the flower, the sapling – in that place in yourself, or your life which feels ugly. Imagine yourself receiving that symbol into your open hands, or placing that symbol in your life, as you would plant in the soil.

Gradually, as you breathe gently, see that beauty coming to maturity; see the bud unfolding in perfection; see the tree growing strong and lovely in the sunlight. Now take your mind back to the ugliness you perceived in yourself or your life and see it transformed. In whatever way is appropriate, see the change from ugliness to beauty, not necessarily a change in form, but certainly a change within your perception.

Hold on to that thought during your daily life, and whenever you feel the sadness or criticism of ugliness creeping in, picture the flower or the tree in full radiance, and know that this is the spiritual truth behind all the illusion of earthliness and karma.

Week Three, Day 4: Rising in Consciousness

Mountain Climbing

Begin by becoming aware of your feet. If it is warm enough, feel the floor, earth or carpet with your bare feet – the sensation of toes wriggling, the firm or soft surface, and how the foot moves on the ground as you put weight on it. Close your eyes and feel the sensation of rolling your feet on the ground.

Imagine you are standing, feeling the strength of your legs and the solidity of the earth; standing at the beginning of a path which snakes up a mountain. Picture the surface of the path and how it would feel to your bare feet. Picture what lies by the side of the path – the vegetation, bushes, flowers, trees and rocks, maybe even a stream. Hear the sound it makes, and the wind through the rocks and the birds soaring over-head, and begin your walk up this path.

In your imagination there is no effort needed, no feelings of discomfort or fear, just the sense of movement upwards in the clear air, and how everything becomes more vivid as you walk. The air has a luminous quality, and you seem to see further and better. As you walk, you are ascending in consciousness towards a golden peak, bathed in the light of the sun, which draws you like a magnet – there is a vibration which flows down towards you, along with the breeze, which is drawing you towards that pinnacle of light, where your vision opens.

Week Three, Day 5: Learning and Growing

Embodying the Highest Self

Begin by thinking of anything which you feel is getting in the way of you embodying your highest self. You may even write these things down – but if you do, remember that an important part of this process is to let go of any sense of wrongdoing, blaming of the self, or criticism. Remember that earthly life is a learning ground, and as such mistakes, wrong turnings, wanderings in the dark are inevitable. Your self-acceptance is the light which will bring you back on track.

Close your eyes and picture yourself seated in a circular chapel with a central altar. On that altar burns an eternal flame, which is the love of God encapsulated for now in this divine fire. As such it is wholly unconditional, wholly capable of the transformation of any energy into the light of the spir-it. Whatever you have written on the paper, or thought about yourself, this flame can transform, and give back to you in a ra-diance which is pure loving comfort and respect for your path.

In your mind, take the paper or the thoughts and place them in the flame on the altar, with the sure knowledge that there is nothing which is outside God's love. As you do so, see and feel a wave of energy flowing to you, stimulating your own heart, releasing the past, and preparing the way ahead.

Week Three, Day 6: At the Heart

Lotus Light

Once you are still and centred, begin with chanting an AUM. As you chant, be aware that something is happening to your vibration – it is changing, expanding and your consciousness is rising.

Picture, as White Eagle described on p. 124, a garden and yourself walking there, and the sensation of the grass under your feet. Soon, you come to a still pool at the centre of the garden, upon which the lily rests in the light of the sun.

Feel that your body is like that still pool. Scan it now and feel all the muscles spreading out, giving you the feeling of water, smoothing and stilling. As you gaze at the pool, have the thought that it is your mind, so that all disturbance, thought, is released until your mind becomes as clear and unruffled as the surface of this pool.

As you gaze at the lily with its golden centre, imagine that it is your heart chakra – an exquisite bloom, open, receptive to the light, and radiating love and the perfume of heaven from its centre.

Week Three, Day 7: Reflection Day

Week Four, Day 1: Moving

Moving Slowly

Rest the backs of your hands in your lap, or beside you on the bed if you are lying down. Take three conscious breaths, and as you breathe in allow your hands very slowly to rise up. As you breathe out move them slowly back down.

On the next three inbreaths, allow the hands to rise slowly upwards and outwards to the side; on the outbreaths let them come back slowly in and down to your lap. Feel the heart opening as the arms move out to the side.

If it feels comfortable to do so, repeat these very slow movements with the breath for some minutes, as long as you wish, perhaps with the thought of being open and receptive to God's love.

Week Four, Day 2: Feeling

Remembering Love

As you enter meditation, imagine a love reaching out to you which is infinitely greater than that which you have felt − a love without judgment or limitation. Feel yourself loved, comforted and uplifted. This love is so powerful it can lift you beyond the fears and limitations of your earthly body and mind. Indeed, at this moment your angel will be surrounding you with an aura so connected to spiritual love that you will be raised in consciousness, whether you are aware of it or not. Love is so potent that it draws love to itself.

Expanding your awareness, imagine the world of spirit where all is love, beauty, peace, strength, understanding and joy. Your guide or master will be there for you if you wish, but it does not matter if you cannot see them, or your vision is hazy or only comes in flashes. In this meditation it is all about exploring the spiritual feeling of your unlimited, spiritual self. Whatever feeling you need, allow yourself to experience it. Imagine yourself being enfolded in it; or that feeling being radiated to you by your guide. What would make you feel most loved, most at peace, most strong? What would lift your heart with its beauty or joy? What would most bring you understanding? Whatever your answer it will be there for you – flowing to you.

Week Four, Day 3: Chanting

Chanting the AUM

As we saw before, White Eagle is very clear that it is important to be in a place where you will not be disturbed in order to safely chant the AUM (OM). This is because of the power that chanting this word from the heart can have on the chakra, on the etheric body and on the mind.

Before beginning your chanting, attune yourself to selfless love, as White Eagle describes it: 'As you become attuned to a beautiful vibration through that selfless love, you will hear within yourself, so that the self within becomes a part of the greater self, of the universal self, the God life, the life spirit of the universe. You will then hear the great word … the AUM: A…U…M. Hear the pulsating word, life-giving, healing, raising you into the spheres of light.'

You raise your consciousness to become attuned in this way through your compassion for people, animals, the Earth herself, or your love for God. Allow your feelings to be moved beyond earthly emotion to the place of deep devotion and divine understanding. As you attune to divine love, so you will be in the right frame of mind to approach your chanting.

The sound is a triple one – made up of three separate 'seed' syllables, so that A … U … and M… are given equal weight and time on each breath. They sound like OM when they are sung together. But, as has been said, this is not so important as where your inward focus lies.

If it helps, you could imagine being part of a circle of monks, who are all chanting with you. Imagine that the sound you make is coming from the spiritual self within. It is not dependent on whether you think you can sing, whether you have chanted before, or how you make the sound. It is your own higher truth, and no matter how it outwardly sounds, it is a free, pure and beautiful spiritual vibration from your heart, which allows the angels of creativity and healing to draw close.

When you finish chanting – the number of times depends on how you feel – allow the silence to grow for a while, so that the inner vibration of creative life which the sounds convey can continue to be felt in every cell of your body, in every part of your being.

Week Four, Day 4: Accepting

Being Now

As you begin this process, with your eyes closed be aware of everything around you – the smells, the sounds, the people, the noise, how the air feels.

It is so easy to be irritated at times when life isn't perfect; when we are not able to be in a sanctified, quiet space dedicated to meditation. Noises intrude, sometimes people intrude.

The thing to do is not to resist any of what is happening around you, but embrace it inwardly. See all that is there in your life now, and in yourself – including any negative responses – as a place to reconnect with love. White Eagle tells us that any feeling of love lifts the consciousness (and the reverse of course happens too). So where there is any resistance, any negative thought or irritation – turn it to love. See it as an opportunity to hold the person who may be making the noise, for instance, in the light and surround them with God's love – even if you cannot feel love yourself at that moment.

Accept this moment now, and from it you will be able to rise in consciousness and be a magnet for the inner world of love.

Week Four, Day 5: Connecting

Walking with your Master

Enter your meditation with the expectation that your master will join you and walk with you, even if you cannot see him. Trust is a crucial part of the meditative process.

Imagine what your master would look like: what they might be wearing, how they would deport themselves, the look in their eyes. Your master will have had many earthly lives and can appear in any one of a number of 'dresses'. Indeed it can be that he or she take on a different 'dress' from the usual one from time to time, for the purpose of helping you.

You will, however, always recognize them from the particular aura they bring; the feeling you get when they are close by. Imagine that feeling now. Also remember that to reach mastery is to reach the place of spontaneous unconditional love. In other words there will be no hint of criticism or disapproval in your master's being ... only complete respect and love and fellow-feeling.

Just as in physical life, it may help to imagine walking through a gateway into the garden of the spirit where you will meet your master. Perhaps just inside the gate you see foot-prints in the dew on the grass, leading off into the bliss of this perfect landscape. Walk in the footsteps of your master for a while, feeling the soft turf, the warmth beneath your bare feet.

These footsteps are leading you into the depths of the gar-den, but really this is an etheric metaphor for your conscious-ness being raised with each step. As you focus on where you place your feet, so the mind loses its busy-ness with outward things, and the love your feel for your master draws you onto a different level of awareness.

There will come a point when you will perceive, or feel, the master waiting for you, either to walk further side by side, or to sit together in communion heart to heart.

This is a being who knows you, and has known you through many lifetimes, and who sees you deep down, not all the surface construction still taking place, but the temple of your soul which is being built through all the trials and mis-takes of life. The master holds the vision of your perfection, and helps you to unveil it to yourself.

Week Four, Day 6: Radiating

Radiating the Love of a Master Soul

We all have situations from time to time, whether personal or ones we are aware of in the world, where it is difficult to love all involved. We are told that to radiate Christ light from our hearts is the greatest help, but because of other feelings it is not always easy.

Think of yesterday's exercise and especially try to feel

again the quality of a master's love – how strong and unconditional that love would be; how that love would be aware of all, would have a complete perspective – so that the true need of all souls would be known.

Imagine the master's love radiating through you to those challenging situations. Let the angels of healing and the master of love use your willingness, even when you cannot feel it yourself.

Visualize that being of light radiating their love to you and through you, and trust that the increase of light will be an opportunity for all to benefit and respond.

Week Four, Day 7: Reflection Day

Week Five, Day 1: Being Still

The Point of Stillness

As you close your eyes think of approaching an actual point of stillness that exists behind and between your eyes, and at a place in your consciousness. It is a point around which all that happens continues, but in the centre of which, like the eye of a storm, all is completely still – the mind, the emotions and the body.

As you breathe, gently and with awareness, feel you are entering that one single point; each inbreath brings you to it, each outbreath brings you to it, until the breath is forgotten and you are just there in the stillness.

Week Five, Day 2: Resting upright

Resting into the Invisible

When you are seated comfortably, or lying on a firm support, take your awareness to a place just below the back of your skull, to the top of your neck. Feel that you can soften there, and let that sensation travel down the neck, so that the neck muscles release and become slack.

As you do this, feel also that the whole of the neck from the base of the skull broadens out to the sides, and that sensation goes all the way down the back...broadening, spreading, softening.

As this happens you may find yourself automatically taking a deeper breath...the chest will lift and open a little more, and the shoulder blades will drop. The whole back of the body is now released.

Then the front of the body rests back against the back; the chest is spread, but not tight. The throat is calm, the muscles of the face spread out to the sides, the eyes deepen in their sockets, and the gaze becomes calm and relaxed.

The whole front of the body is resting back against the back; the whole self moves away from force, action, forward-seeking and striving, and relaxes back into trust; into the support of the inner spine.

Week Five, Day 3: Focusing

Beginning to Really Listen, to See
and to be Aware of Scent and Touch

Take a walk, sit, or lie outside, or with a window open, and listen to the sound the wind makes in the trees, or to the birds ... this is sound vibration. Feel that sound of the wind not only as something your brain interprets as sound, but as a vibration which passes through you and affects every particle of yourself. Imagine the cells of the body vibrating in and with the wind.

All life is vibration.

If there is no wind, look at the colours around you, colour vibration, or take a few conscious breaths and be aware of the scents. Again, be aware of these vibrations as not only visible, or understood by the brain, but as vibration which moves every cell; influences your whole body and all your auras.

Week Five, Day 4: Rising

Float Upwards

Practise straw breathing (see p. 40) for a while , breathing in through the nose quite normally and out through pursed lips. Be aware that you are breathing not just air, but prana, chi, the life force, God.

After a while, feeling that with every inbreath you become lighter, and with every outbreath you rise upwards. Have an image of a feather floating down to earth slowly moving from side to side, and imagine yourself with each breath floating upwards – gravity reversed – in just the same way. An inner awareness may grow of your consciousness being raised through all the planes of life to the highest in the gentle movement of the breath of God within.

Week Five, Day 5: Experiencing

The Infinite and Eternal Garden

Read what White Eagle says in the paragraphs below, and then use any aspect which appeals to you to create your perfect garden, or natural scene in your mind. You will find the mind wanders, so choose one object or sensation which you can return to each time the mind has wandered off. (Of course, you might find you wander off into that garden, which will be delightful!)

'In this method of meditation, after we have made that initial contact in the golden light at the apex of the mountain, you are instructed to use the creative imagination in order to visualize in the soul world a most perfect and beautiful garden – the infinite and eternal garden.

'In creating a garden in the inner worlds, we have a wide choice of season and setting. For instance, it may be spring-time in your garden, or high summer with all its rich colour and life; we might see the garden set in a perfect landscape with majestic trees, flowering shrubs and herbaceous borders; or with rock gardens and a running brook of pure clear water through which can be seen stones like jewels, and fish of differ-ent colours. There may be smooth green lawns, or a blue lake.

'In these surroundings we are able to use our creative im-agination to develop our spiritual senses. As we observe the light and life in all the beautiful form, we develop our spiritual senses of sight and sound as we listen to the song of birds, the trickle of water in the brooks and waterfalls, the music of the gentle wind in the trees. We can develop our spiritual sense of smell as we inhale the pungent freshness of the earth and the subtle perfumes of the variety of flowers, some of which may be unknown to us on earth. We develop too our spiritual sense of taste as in imagination we try the fruit from bush, tree and vine, and cup our hands to sip the fresh sweet water. We can explore our sense of touch as our hands are immersed in that cool water, or laid upon the living stones which edge the lily pool.'

Week Five, Day 6: Radiating

At the Garden's Heart

Seek to recreate in your mind the garden you visited in yes-terday's attunement. White Eagle has many times referred to the lily or lotus pool which can be found at its heart. At the centre of this pool is a beautiful bloom, resting on the water among the leaves.

At the heart of this bloom is a radiance as bright as the

sun. The pool represents the stilled emotions and mind. The lily is your heart chakra – the centre for the highest form of love.

What do you long to do when you love? You long to give, and so here in this garden of the spirit, the heart of the lotus, the heart of your being, with each outbreath you radiate peace, beauty, healing and the blessing of the Christ love within to all.

Week Five, Day 7: Reflection Day

Week Six, Day 1: Flowing

Watching the Waves

As you prepare with gentle awareness of the breath, feel the rise and fall of your chest, as well as the expansion and retraction of the ribcage. This is a wave-like motion which is natural and easy, just like the waves flowing onto a beach and retreating back. As you feel this movement of your body, perhaps you will see in your mind's eye a beach of golden sand and a blue-green sea stretching to the horizon. With each breath, the white-capped waves roll in and out, while the earth is still, receiving the blessing and giving it back to the ocean.

Have the feeling that what you are watching and feeling is the breath of God within you. It's the flow of *prana* – or if you prefer, *chi* – or just light, which continuously fills your life, and can pass from you in blessing and healing to all.

Week Six, Day 2: Letting Go

Surrender and Grace

Think of something in yourself you wish to surrender. You may wish to surrender to something which is happening in your life, or to surrender something.

Picture the cross within the circle: as White Eagle says, 'the symbol of that ray of light which inspired John is the equal-sided cross within the circle – the symbol of surrender of the self into the circle of eternal love, which alone brings true wisdom.' Imagine yourself at the heart of that cross, placing yourself, or that which you wish to surrender, there.

Now see that there is a star of divine grace at the heart of the cross within the circle, and imagine what would flow back to you from that star as a result of this surrender. It will be different for each person – it may be a quality, an opportunity, or a change in relationship with someone or something.

Accept this grace by being as you imagine you would be as a result of receiving this, even if it does not immediately appear to be happening outwardly. Remember, things happen etherically before they happen physically, and take time to work through to the outer awareness.

Week Six, Day 3: Imagining

The Lotus of the Self

The lotus is symbolic of the heart chakra, but we can also see it as a representation of our whole self. The roots reach down into the rich earth of human experience. The stem is surrounded by the water of our emotional responses to what we encounter in daily life. The flower holds itself above these waters in pure air with focused purpose, and then opens to the fire of the sun, the light, the warmth and God's love.

All the elements are represented here: earth, water, air, fire. White Eagle does not say that ether is separate from these, but rather that there is an etheric counterpart to earth, water, air and fire. It is the etheric which links us with our soul and spirit. So the most perfect expression of all these elements will produce, eventually, the fully-evolved flower of the God self.

The earth brings to our roots nourishment and steadiness. It brings us the opportunities to make choices. The water brings us the chance to develop poise amid the changing circumstances of life – and for the lotus to grow, the water needs to be still. The air brings clarity, it allows the light through; the air needs to be pure in order to offer a lucid focus for the sun's rays. The fire of the sun draws forth our own warmth and love.

The pattern of growth is also important. We have to learn all about the earth, otherwise we would not be grounded and receptive. The stem grows strong through this, strong to withstand any buffeting of the waters flowing around us. But once that bud reaches the air it does not rest on the surface of the water but lifts itself above the emotional state into a realm of purity of mind, where it can open unimpeded and fully to the Sun.

As well as this, what actually causes the lotus to grow? White Eagle says we contain the seed atom of God within us, which is the Christ child, a reflection of God's light. The warmth of the Sun sets up a resonance which is felt within every cell of the body of the plant or of us, and calls forth that seed atom to arise and grow towards the Light.

That arisen self is the Christ within, called forth by the Father (Sun); nurtured and given what it needs to grow by the Mother (Earth).

Week Six, Day 4: The Highest

Steps Across the Bridge

Begin by feeling your feet on the floor, or by taking a short walk and being aware of the sensations more than you usually would. So you feel toes, heels, firmness of ground or floor supporting you – the feeling of smooth floor or rough ground.

If you've walked a short way, come back to your chair, but still keep your focus on your feet. Close your eyes and imagine that you stand before a bridge of light which extends into the hazy distance. Feel the sensation in your feet of standing ready to cross that bridge. The feet are your understanding. Allow the understanding of this inner world of love – of home – to carry you forward onto the bridge. It's a sensation of floating, hardly touching, yet clearly moving into the light.

As you cross the etheric bridge the mist rolls away and you are walking into the radiance and beauty of the inner world, drawn by the sounds of laughter, the scents of summer and the aura of peace and tender welcome.

Week Six, Day 5: Meeting

Finding the Seat

Begin by being aware of how you are seated. Feel the physical chair beneath you, the feet on the floor, how the hands rest in your lap. Then take your thoughts back to yesterday and the etheric bridge stretching out before you into the distance. This time, with each breath feel yourself moving. Breathe out and take a step towards the light at the end of the bridge. Breathe in and feel that light drawing closer to you.

At the end of the bridge this time is the archway of light you entered on week one, and, as you move through it, the garden you may now be familiar with opens out before you. Not all gardens are the same, of course, so this is above all a place that appeals to you – it may be a forest, a moorland, a mountain by the sea, a snowy landscape, or an orchard of blossoming spring trees.

Somewhere not far away there is a seat. Finding it, you sit and continue breathing in the sweet, fresh air – feeling as you do so that your consciousness is raised just a little more, until you can see someone coming to sit with you in communion, heart to heart.

Don't worry about visualizing – that will come in time – just feel them next to you – maybe a hand in yours or an arm around you, and know they are very much alive in this garden of reunion.

Week Six, Day 6: Heart Mind

Lifting the Thoughts into Clarity and Beauty

To begin this meditation, focus on breathing in the light, perhaps with the thought: *I breathe in light, I breathe out peace.* Feel the heart centre of divine love expanding in light with each breath.

And as previously, visualize the light in the form of a flame, the radiance from which gradually reaches up to the brow. As you focus on the brow, bringing your inner attention to that chakra just above and between the eyes, imagine a clear diamond resting there, and the light from the flame penetrating and reflecting from the beautiful, clear crystal surfaces.

Feel your mind becoming and more and more still, until 'the transparent radiance of the stilled mind' takes over your consciousness, and you are raised into the higher mental world of true vision.

Week Six, Day 7: Reflection Day

Week Seven, Day 1: No Expectations

Creating Mental Space

Imagine yourself standing or sitting in a light but empty room with French windows, open to the garden beyond. It is summer, and the scents of flowers and grass flow into the room. There is space all around, and a sense of freedom, with the garden full of soaring birds and a backdrop of hills against the wide open sky.

There is no clutter anywhere, no expectations on your time, no things to worry about. As you breathe in the sweet air coming from the garden, allow that there is space between each breath, and as you do this allow that there is also space between your thoughts.

Week Seven, Day 2: Centring

The Smile of the Buddha

Use the exercise of week two, day 1 (p. 187) to have the feeling of the rod of light of your inner spine. Feel your back is straight and strong and imagine that rod of light reaching down through the crown and into the earth, centring you.

Picture an image of a Thai Buddha – the incredibly straight, yet relaxed back rising up from the firm lotus position. See how the hands rest in his lap and how broad the chest is as the spine reaches up – the heart open to life. Try to feel that within yourself.

Picture the Buddha's head, balanced without strain –

the chin level, the brow spreading, the crown open, and the mouth showing that enigmatic smile – a smile which radiates tranquillity, insists that all is well.

Feel that for yourself – copy the Buddha's smile and allow the endorphins and finer vibrations that go with them to fill the physical body with healing and peace.

Week Seven, Day 3: Being Aware

Seeing the Spiritual Life Force in Nature

If you can, take a gentle walk somewhere you love, and when ready choose a part of the scenery around you as your focal point. Whatever natural phenomenon is the subject of your focus, choose something beautiful to you, and have the intention in your mind that you will be 'seeing' the light, or life force, within nature.

In the world of spirit, in the gardens there, one is aware of every blade of grass, leaf and stem shining with an inner light, which seems to extend outwards, but doesn't mask the beauty of the colour, rather enhances it – something like the light through stained glass windows. As you contemplate your natural world, have in your mind's eye this idea.

Imagine what this would look like. Imagine the light radiating out beyond the plant a little, like an aura. Focus on one aspect of nature, and try to relax the mind, so that you enter a dreamy state where all is possible – and of course it is not only possible, but it is there.

When you can do this, if only for a fraction of time, you will be entering a state in which you can also become aware of the agents of that life force, the elementals and the angels of form. Have faith that they are there, and gradually in that light you may glimpse movement, or you may instead feel sudden joy, which is one of the feelings which the nature spirits bring.

Week Seven, Day 4: Mountain Climbing

Your Sacred Space

There are places which feel very special to us – as if the atmosphere is so pure that we sense something beyond the physical there.

Remember or create such a place in your thoughts. If you like, describe it to yourself out loud as if you were telling a good friend about it. Describe where it is, what it looks like, and the quality of vibration, but most of all describe what it feels like inside, within the boundaries of wall, stones, tree, shelter.

Imagine stepping into that place once more and finding the vibration is even more real, even stronger. Imagine what is happening to your aura – the blending of your consciousness with the higher essence of this inner sanctuary. It is your own most sacred space.

Week Seven, Day 5: Learning and Growing

Far Memories – Soul Memories

Revisit your sacred space from yesterday. If you wrote down your experiences, read what you've written, or otherwise recreate in your mind both the place and the special vibration which works for you – it may be peace or beauty, natural scenes or grandeur.

Imagine stepping into this inner sanctuary once more,

and in the centre find a table, stone or altar, upon which is a flame. This flame is quite still, and glows golden white, its radiance filling the space with a vibration of intense peace.

Sit and breathe in the serenity from the flame. Feel it penetrating your aura, your mind and soul with every breath. As the flame rises upwards, let your consciousness rise as well; imagine it lifting into the higher mental world where all the soul's positive memories still exist. The more still you are able to be at this point, if there is a far memory which your higher self needs to revisit, now is the moment. It may only be fleeting, or come to you in snatches, but most important will be the vibration it brings – an energy or perhaps a particular quality that you are reconnecting with.

As you come out of this meditative state, breathe that quality back into your physical body-self.

Week Seven, Day 6: Reflecting

Meditation for Dispassion

You are met in the garden by a seated figure: a Buddhist monk sitting simply on the grass. He looks up and smiles and this is an invitation for you to sit with him. You sit opposite him and see that in his hands he holds a simple white lotus bloom, which you contemplate with him in the silence. After a while, he puts the lotus down on a small pool which appears between you, and then raindrops begin to fall, dappling the surface of the pool.

You sit on in silence and stillness, and he teaches you the lesson of non-resistance and equanimity in the face of all. Your attention may be drawn outwards to the sounds around you, and the sensations and thoughts of the body, but you feel you could experience the stillness and silence underneath any noise, or sensation.

In that silence you may experience your true self, free from limitation. You may feel greater, more aware on many levels. As you return to complete earthly consciousness, you earth this awareness and this ability to be more than you think you are.

Week Seven, Day 7: Reflection Day

Week Eight, Day 1: Centring

Mindful Movement

For this exercise there is no need to do anything except decide for a while to move mindfully about your daily tasks – not exactly slowly, but so that whatever you are doing is done with deliberation and mindfully. You are seeking to be wholly present in the movements you make, and therefore wholly present with the inner consciousness of the moment.

The important part is not to rush anything. So much of what we do is fast and without thought, which means that when we try to sit still it is an effort.

Be aware of what you are doing, but without slowing down to the degree it becomes unnatural, or uncomfortable. Be aware of each movement without becoming self-obsessed. Gradually you will find that you become more and more centred. Extraneous actions are sloughed off, any irritations dissolve, and you reconnect with thankfulness for every moment of your life.

Week Eight, Day 2: Releasing

The Grail Cup

One of the great skills of meditation is being able to empty oneself of all preconceptions, preoccupations and anything which will get in the way of the consciousness being raised. It is often a deliberate process of releasing. As you sit quietly at the beginning of your meditation time, you may be aware of tensions in the body and thoughts spinning in the mind. It is not very easy to empty the mind completely; in fact, White Eagle says it is not really possible, but we can learn to choose our focus, and set the mind on spiritual rather than earthly things.

Picture a grail cup and imagine that you are that cup – indeed that every cell in your body is part of that holy receptacle. This is the point at which you have the intention to release as a deliberate act, so have the thought that with each outbreath the cup is emptying – all physical, unimportant things are draining out of you. You may indeed have the sensation of release and of opening out, the awareness of creating space within yourself.

Allow yourself to spread out into that space. Each outbreath is an opportunity to create and occupy that space within yourself, to let go of blockages and to reveal the golden chalice of the self, still radiant and open to receive.

And now you can be aware of the light of God pouring down into the chalice of the self, filling every part with the eternal love of the spirit. As you become filled with this spiritual essence, so your consciousness changes and your spiritual senses awaken.

Week Eight, Day 3: Chanting

Harmonizing with the Divine

As you sit quietly in preparation for meditation, imagine you are listening to the AUM being chanted in the distance and gradually drawing closer to you. You hear the distinct sounds of the chant, A ... U ... MMMM.

As you imagine this chant, think of it as sounding with the highest love you can conceive; a power so great that it is beyond earthly things, and yet something which your deepest heart recognizes as being the source of your life.

Take a few 'straw' breaths (see p. 40,) and when you are ready join in with the chant you 'hear' in your mind, while focusing in your mind and heart on that Divine Source.

Feel your whole being responding to that sound, which vibrates in every cell of your body and in all your auras. Try not to judge the quality of the sound with the earthly mind – in spirit it will be heard as a perfect expression of your heart.

Repeat the AUM for as long as you wish. It can be a meditation in itself, or lead into a deep silence, or an opening of the inner vision – it will bring whatever is your soul's need for your individual self at this moment.

Week Eight, Day 4: Feeling

Etheric Fountain

As you sit in the stillness, remember what it is like to take a shower after a busy day. Remember the sensation of warm water cascading down so that you feel clean, refreshed.

Then imagine standing before a fountain which is not just water, but light-filled water of the spirit. Look at the play of light and feel the slight movement of the air as the water drops through it – the air being refreshed so that as you breathe it in it is like being by the sea, breathing in the sea air.

Then, keeping your memory of the sensation of showering, step under the fountain and feel not a wetness of the body so much as a complete refreshing of your aura. Imagine droplets of light falling through the aura (which interpenetrates the whole physical body).

As this aura cleansing continues, if there is a particular need, you may be aware of the fountain changing to a certain colour, which feeds and strengthens your etheric body and right through to the physical.

Week Eight, Day 5: Connecting

Meditation Leading to the Angelic Sphere

Make yourself so comfortable in your chair that you will not need to move at all: upright, and with cushions behind the back if needed. This comfort is vital so that all movement in the body can cease, and then the physical nervous system relaxes and the etheric takes over.

Deliberately relax your muscles, especially those of the shoulders and the neck, keeping the spine lifted and the chest open if you can, or have that in your mind as a vision of perfection. Images or statues of Thai Buddhas should give you that position to emulate.

As you become more still, allow your mind to believe that you can and are entering the aura of the angels. Ask your own angel to guide you if you wish. That guidance will take the form of an enveloping, deepening quietude.

You may not see anything, and it is best not to expect to see, because the mind will get busy with form. Rather, experience with your whole being a sense of being held in space and time, cocooned, centred in the core of beingness, without being anything specific.

If you think of anything, think of being aware and being all. No matter whether you are aware of this or not, the angelic level of consciousness will have been reached through the profundity of your stillness and acknowledgment of the existence of another level of reality. This is the handle of the door, which is always on our side.

Week Eight, Day 6: Radiating

The Throat Chakra

White Eagle says this of the throat chakra: 'All these colours have an etheric vibration – an aspect of love – as well as the physical ones'.

Spend a little time remembering what the compassion of the master feels like as you may have experienced it in Week four, days 5 and 6 (pp. 206-8); the wider perspective that understands all needs, and the causes of all suffering in the world, both personal and national.

Feel your heart chakra expanding as you focus on that all-encompassing love, and the suffering of the world. Your aura is extending and the Christ love in your heart is beginning to animate all the other chakras.

With each breath, imagine your heart's love rising up the rod of light of the inner spine to your throat centre – the seat of creation – which is beginning to revolve and send out beautiful colours.

Begin again to sound the AUM, either silently or outwardly, and as the sound flows, so the angels are using your higher thoughts and the vibrations of the sound, so that healing, peace, love and compassion are flowing to all people, all creatures, to the earth herself; wherever there is need.

Week Eight, Day 7: Reflection Day

Appendix Two:
When It is Difficult

SOMETIMES meditating can be difficult, no matter how experienced we are. This may be disheartening and at the beginning it may cause people to think they are at fault, and to give up. This section is designed to reassure you whenever you are going through one of these periods of drought and doubt, and to offer some suggestions.

White Eagle was once asked: 'How is it that there are times when there is a sheen of happiness over everything, and there are others when the heavens seem as brass and the soul can make no effort to overcome this condition?'

This was his reply: 'My child, this experience comes to almost every soul. Perhaps it is even more familiar to the soul that has received a certain amount of illumination. When you have been caught up into the heavens, it is all the more bitter to come down and remain on earth. You cannot get back into heaven. Now, the thing to do is to learn to accept that condition patiently. Do you remember Moses, who wandered in the wilderness for forty days? It was his period of darkness. You may be like that for forty hours, days, or even forty years. You may have this experience often or infrequently.

These periods usually follow a time of great exaltation, when you have felt, 'Now I know truth. Life will always be different.' But there will be periods when your soul is going through the lesser night (we are not referring to the great night of darkness). Once you learn to accept that condition tranquilly as being part of your training, part of the divine plan, something arises in you which we will call the 'lesser light' to illumine your path. If you kick against the pricks, if you become agitated and turn away from the spiritual path because of this apparent darkness, then you will not learn the lesson which the condition is intended to bring you. Try to accept it tranquilly. Do not worry. Go on with your work. Take no notice. The lesser light, the light of the moon, companions you; this 'lesser light' is your confidence and faith, even if you cannot see that the light is there, for it may be behind a cloud. The aspirant will always have these times when the heavens seem as brass but this inward knowledge, this certainty, which we call the lesser light, the light of the moon, will teach you to be still, to be patient, and not to force the issue.'

Once I was part of a conversation with a psychiatrist who understands the benefits of meditation, and who works with people suffering from Post-Traumatic Stress (PTS). He related that for some time after a person undergoes trauma, meditating can be very difficult. This is because when the person sits still in the silence, all the memories and flashbacks surface, and the mind gets on the treadmill of anxious thoughts.

Most readers may never, thankfully, have to experience such trauma, but we all undergo periods of stress, and the effects and processes in the brain are the same. We may not have flashbacks, but we all know the problem of an overactive mind, which will not let go of the past and future worrying due to that often-unrecognized stress.

As White Eagle has said, the first thing to do is to accept where we are and not force ourselves to meditate. For this reason here is a list instead of a whole variety of activities:
- Indoor or outdoor climbing or bouldering.
- Life painting.
- Taking part in a conversation class in a language not your first.

- Knitting using a complicated pattern.
- Under safe conditions, driving or cycling off-road on rough terrain.
- Following a complicated recipe.
- Teaching someone how to do something.
- Taking part in any team sport at any level.
- Playing video games which require manual dexterity and focus.

In order to give our brains a chance to switch off from the merry-go-round of thought and the consequent stress, the activity we engage in needs to be something upon which we have to focus hard to avoid failure or disaster.

When We are Ready

There will come a point when a person feels ready to meditate again. Then we would suggest you start with any of the exercises which have a physical reference: those which involve movement like walking, chanting, breathing. In such a way, we are helping ourself to move on in a way which focuses the mind first and foremost, before we are happy to let go into the silence.

Appendix Three: A Summary of the Characteristics of White Eagle Meditation

Aspire

One of the keynotes of this form of meditation is that it begins with aspiration to God – to the greatest source of all goodness, love, wisdom and creative power that we can conceive. This then raises the consciousness above not only the earthly level, but also above the tumult of the astral and lower mental levels of life, which surround the physical. This highest aspiration connects us with the spiritual spheres.

So we might begin a meditation with a piece of inspiring music, or words from White Eagle, which will give the opportunity to turn thoughts and feelings away from the worries and distress of physical life and bring our vibration towards a place of harmony and spiritual aspiration.

Align the Body with the Spirit

Along with this comes an awareness of how the body is positioned, in order to maximize the aspiration – that is, with the spine straight, so that the chakras are aligned and the will is strengthened, yet the body remains firmly and safely earthed. We are not seeking to leave the body, neither to experience astral projection, or occult experiences.

Use the Breath

We seek to create a condition of stillness and peace of mind, body and emotions. This might be achieved by rhythmic God-breathing – an awareness of our breathing in not only air, but the spiritual life-force, and with each outbreath attempting to surrender the earthly self and concerns.

Visualize

In meditation we are asked not only to aspire towards spiritual things, but to visualize them as well: to create an image in our minds which, in its loveliness and loving purpose, will form a bridge. This bridge is then the means by which we are enabled to raise our vibration to the higher levels and is the means by which that inner world may become manifest.

Create the Focal Point

We imagine a focal point for the awareness. This could be as simple an image as a still white flame, or a rose opening in the light of the sun. Focusing on such an image, the mind and emotions can be brought to a point of stillness and poise, as is the body. Additionally, the image itself is one which evokes a spiritual response, albeit subtle and often unconscious, in us.

Consciousness is Raised

In all these ways our consciousness is being raised or heightened. Another way of putting it is that our whole vibration is being raised; our brainwaves are changing, and thus we are becoming more receptive to the subtle, higher energies of the spiritual consciousness.

In such a state we can begin to function on a different level – begin to use senses which are the equivalent of the earthly senses, but on a higher octave, so to speak. We might call them spiritual senses, ones with which we can experience the spiritual world while we are still on earth. From the focal point at the beginning of the meditation, other images, feelings and awarenesses may evolve, particularly as we become more experienced in being still and receptive. It is thus that we can catch glimpses of past lives, make a true contact with those in spirit, and be reminded of the spiritual wisdom, power and love which guides and guards us all. Even by remaining focused on the initial image we can find that deeper feelings of peace and clarity, for example, begin to be present – we are becoming spiritually aware, and thus transcending the limits of the earthly personality.

Transformation

This contact, no matter how fleeting, is transforming. Not only does it consciously remind those who practise meditation of why we are here and help us to make sense of our lives, but it helps and encourages us to live lovingly and creatively for good. A true contact with the spiritual spheres of existence is wholly good and constructive, since the first aspiration has been towards God.

From the first moment we aspire to meditate in this way, no matter how limited our success appears to be, things are changed within us. We may not see or feel any different at first; it may be hard to visualize, or to trust the imagination; it may be difficult to sit still, and to keep the mind focused gently on the image. Nevertheless, the change in vibration and consciousness begins to happen because of our aspirations, and our desire to raise our thoughts and feelings to a place of true beauty, wisdom and peace. The very thought is enough, which may be one reason why there are so many reports of people spontaneously experiencing meditative states while they are out in nature, when their minds and feelings are lifted by the scenes they witness.

Serve

White Eagle meditation always involves some aspect of service, which is an important part of the work of the White

Eagle Lodge. In a simple way we might use the adage 'as you give you receive' to explain this. White Eagle tells us that this statement is a 'spiritual law of life'. But it is not in order to receive that we send out loving thoughts and light to those in need, rather, it spontaneously happens! When in meditating we 'touch' the spirit, we are reconnected with unconditional love and the deepest compassion for suffering in any form. It is then that we long to give, to bring healing and peace, to bring light into the dark corners of the world, and so in this form of meditation, White Eagle teaches us how to send out the light of the Christ star as a way of channelling that natural and spontaneous feeling of love so that it can be used for good.

Complete

At the end of the meditation we seek to come back to earthly consciousness in a gentle way, but firmly. We seal the chakras (see below), which become more receptive while we are meditating, so that we do not feel over-sensitive as we go about our daily life. Through this spiritual contact we can learn not only that we are more than just this earthly being, but also the importance of earthly existence, and of living life thankfully, and to the full.

The Sealing Ritual

At the end of the meditation, see inwardly an image of a cross of light within a circle of light. Imagine this symbol above the crown of the head, between the brows, at the hollow of the throat, at the centre of the chest, at the solar plexus (between the navel and the diaphragm), between the hip bones (sacral centre), and under the base of the spine.

Imagine you are drawing the light up through the aura on the left side of the body as you breathe in, and as you breathe out see the light flowing down the right side from the crown to earth, making a circle of light around the body. Repeat this six times, using the breath.

The last seal is done on just one breath. Imagine the light spiralling up the body clockwise seven times as you breathe in. As you breathe out see the light passing right down from the crown through the centre of the body (the inner etheric spine) to the earth.

Index